THE ULTIMATE LEADER

Learning, Leading and Leaving a Legacy of Hope

By

Brigette Tasha Hyacinth

Book Design by: Giovanni Misagrande

Legal Disclaimer

Paperback ISBN: 978-976-8271-31-0
Hard Cover ISBN: 978-976-8271-29-7
Ebook ISBN: 978-976-8271-30-3

Preface

In the beginning was… Leadership. Nothing begins, develops or changes without leadership, whether it is in our lives, homes, communities, organizations or country. Therefore, leadership is at the helm of a successful society. Our society and every organization would soon collapse if there were no leaders, more precisely wise leaders. In building your leadership skills you need Authenticity, Humility, Integrity and Hope—The Pillars of Leadership. If you build your leadership without anyone of these four pillars, it will eventually crumble. **The Ultimate leader: Learning, Leading and Leaving a Legacy of Hope** is your roadmap to performing at your optimum level. It charts the path forward to creating a lasting legacy.

Table of Contents

SECTION ONE

THE PILLARS OF LEADERSHIP

CHAPTER ONE

HOPE: The Cornerstone
of Leadership

In the 1800's, an Italian intellectual, named Giancomo Leopardi, wrote about the overriding unhappiness of human beings, saying that "as long as man feels life, he also feels displeasure and pain." Hope is the one thing that lifts the human spirit and keeps us going in spite of our difficulties that we face. Hope looks beyond life's hardships to a better, brighter tomorrow. It keeps us believing and expecting that out of today's darkness, tomorrow's light will shine brightly. Hope is seeing the future; a future we can attain if we keep moving forward and, as needed, adjusting and adapting. A leader's hopeful outlook enables people to see beyond today's challenges to tomorrow's answers.

The word hope is derived from the old English word *hopian* and it literally means to "leap forward with expectation." Hope is a real genuine feeling of possibility. It has substance when there is a clear vision and a defined direction. It is more than a wish; an optimistic thought or faith. Maintaining hope has to do with being able to evaluate, recover from discouragement, and hold onto the vision of what can be. It is an emotional magnet that keeps people going even in the midst of challenges.

In 1997, a Nobel Prize-winning physicist made a stir when he wrote, "The more the universe seems comprehensible, the more it seems pointless." Responding to the statement, one astronomer wrote, "Why should it have a point? What point? It's just a physical system; what point is there?" Another scientist, agreeing, said, "I am willing to believe that we are flotsam and jetsam." Flotsam and jetsam?

The Roman statesman, Pliny, once said, "Hope is the pillar that holds up the world." He was correct. Without hope, society would collapse, as we would live our lives in despair. Hope enables us to believe that the future we envision is attainable, and to move toward our visions and goals while inspiring others toward those goals as well.

"Hope is like the sun, which, as we journey toward it, casts the shadow of our burden behind us." —Samuel Smiles

Leadership is about making a difference in people's lives. It's about instilling and managing hope with real opportunities and goals that people believe they can achieve. Leaders today face unprecedented challenges. The twentieth century began in a mood of great optimism. Since the beginning of the Enlightenment Era, optimism had dominated the way of thinking in the Western world. New inventions, new modes of travel, the dramatic increase of medical knowledge, the introduction of new machines would improve all lives. However, life after September 11, 2001 has greatly changed. People will always remember the images of passenger airliners flying into the twin towers of the World Trade Center. We all realize that it can happen again. There is fear everywhere and, considering the world we live in, that fear is understandable. It's easy to understand why. Between 2003 and 2012, there has been an average of 338 devastating natural disasters including earthquakes, tsunamis, hurricanes, and cyclones, just to name a few each year. These disasters have left thousands dead and millions homeless, and have dramatically affected the world economy, costing a massive U.S. $157 billion. Senseless terrorist attacks have created feelings of fear and anxiety in the face of horrific acts of brutality. And, to make matters worse, the world's economy hangs on a thin line. Russian philosopher, Fyodor Dostoyevsky, was undoubtedly right when he said, "To live without hope is to cease to live." The current scientific consensus is that sooner or later, the entire

15

cosmos will diminish and die in what has been called "The Cosmic Heath Death."

According to a CNN/Opinion Research Corporation polling data taken in the United States in 1999, 85 percent of Americans surveyed were hopeful about the future. By December, 2009, the number of those who were hopeful about their personal future had reduced to 69 percent, and only 51 percent were hopeful about the world's future. By 2013, only 40 percent of those polled were hopeful about the world's future. "Necessity," it has been said, "is the mother of invention." The word *mother*, in this case, means "the source," "the driving force," "the foundation." It's the need; the necessity for something that moves people to action. All these negative developments are the driving force behind the need for inspirational leadership.

Murphy's Law is considered by some to be one of the central laws of nature; as universal as gravity and electromagnetism. It states in a nutshell: Whatever can go wrong will go wrong. We all have moments and days that seem to follow Murphy's Law. Sometimes, our experiences can get us down. We should always hold on to hope to help us not get discouraged.A young woman who undertook counselling to recover from a predicament told her friends that one statement conveyed by the counsellor was key to her successful recovery. "What helped me most," she said, "was the counsellor insisting that my agonising situation would come to an end." "It looks gloomy and dark now," the counsellor used to say, "but it will not last much longer. This thought helped me gain resilience." In other words, the counsellor kept the woman's hope alive.

Hope is essential in order to live our lives. A person who is in search of a job must hope that they'll find suitable employment, investors who have lost their money must believe that they will overcome this hurdle, or a lost traveller must hope to find his way back. Living with zero hope leads to depression, and eventually death. When Italian philosopher and poet, Dante Alighieri (1265–1321) attempted to describe hell in his Divine Comedy, he proposed a big sign at the entrance, saying, "Abandon all hope, ye who enter here!" The worst punishment is to deprive someone of hope.

The world's greatest leaders all have one thing in common; they brought hope in the face of despair. The Martin Luther King Jr. "I have a Dream" speech oozes hope. As he addressed the crowd, he acknowledged their plight. "I am not unmindful that some of you have come here out of great trials and tribulations." He kept their eyes on the brighter road ahead. "Let us not wallow in the valley of despair… This is our hope, and this is the faith that I go back to the South with. With this faith, we will be able to hew out of the mountain of despair a stone of hope."

Although he has passed on and most of us never had the opportunity to meet him, his words still continue to inspire millions around the world and that is why we admire leaders like him. They gave us something to hold on to; they made a personal connection with us through giving us hope. "I have a dream that my four little children will one day live in a nation where they will not be judged by the color of their skin, but by the content of their character. I have a dream today!" —Martin Luther King Jr.

"I believe hope is the only thing we can never afford to be without, and the jet fuel for the journey of work and life." —Libby Gill

Hope changes the way we perceive situations. Robert Louis Stevenson, best known for his adventure story, *Treasure Island,* had been a sickly boy who couldn't go to school regularly. Finally, his parents hired a teacher to teach him and a nanny to help with his personal needs. One night, when his nanny came to check on him before he went to bed, he was out of bed and his hands and nose were pressed against the window. His nanny firmly told him to get back in bed before he got a chill.

Robert said to her, "Come to the window and see what I'm seeing."

The nanny came to see. Down below, on the street, there was a lamplighter lighting the streetlights. "Look," said Robert, "a man is poking holes in the darkness!" —Margaret Davis, *Fear Not! Is There Anything Too Hard for God?*

Challenging times like these that we are facing,are the most difficult in which to lead,especially as the workplace changes, the economy struggles, and employees live in fear and uncertainty of their jobs. People are challenged to remain motivated. On top of that, leaders are asking for more and more, which does not directly correlate with an increase in remuneration. Leaders;therefore,need to make a positive impact in people's lives. People are looking for inspiration that speaks to their needs. Employees want to believe again in their leaders, but are continually faced with so much unauthenticated and selfish behaviour. The need for inspirational leadership is at an all-time high. People are tired of false promises and rapid changes that leave them worse off. They want certainty during a time in history when the world is disillusioned by artificial relationships and the constant reminders that things aren't getting much better. In one word, they want **hope**.

It is even more critical that leaders inspire people to give their best. Inspiring a shared vision amid layoffs, downsizing, and radical changes in the way we do business is tough. Much like trust, inspiring hope in others takes time and patience. Emotions are contagious. Employees don't leave their emotions at the door when they report for work. If they are having personal problems, those emotions affect their work. Similarly, no one can sustain constant sacrifice. Almost every organization has been trying to do more with less resources lately, and it's taking a toll on employees. A leader's ability to tap into and know their workers' feelings, and to articulate how he or she is responding to major events in ways that instil confidence and hope are key behaviours that enable leaders to resonate with their people. Leaders deal with people; people bring to the table skills, insight, and emotions. The first two of these may be constants in anyone's day, but it's our emotions that ebb and flow with the circumstances we're faced with. Hope intersects the emotional needs that people have at any given moment;it's not a buzzword or a catchy slogan. Leaders must have a solid Emotional Intelligence to deal with people's emotions. There are many factors, both internal and external, to the organization and the individual that make a person's belief in the mission waver.

One Monday morning, when I came out my office to greet staff however, I noticed many employees were missing. I enquired with management on the floor and it was determined many of them were facing personal problems, which included sickness, death of a family member, ill parents, children issues, financial and relationship problems. It was a dismal atmosphere in the office. Almost everybody was going through something. They were barely hanging on.I realized I had to do more because it was affecting their attendance and subsequent productivity. Our office had to be a place of **Hope**. I wanted them to be inspired and not dread to have to come to work in spite of all the troubles they were facing.

Hope is contagious. The Zambeki River in Zambia, Africa starts as a shallow brook that comes from under a tree. As it flows toward Victoria Falls, it grows from a brook (ankle-deep) to knee-deep, and then to a river that is deep enough to swim in. The same applies to hope.

A wise leader will input hope into the vision and mission of their organization;they will work to make sure that everyone is focused on the task at hand. More importantly, they will make the vision bigger than the obstacles that threaten the mission itself. Giving hope to your team combines the alignment, engagement, and vision of the organization.

Man is the only animal," wrote British essayist William Hazlitt, "that laughs and weeps; for he is the only animal that is struck with the difference between what things are, and what they ought to be." Things certainly may not be what they ought to be but dwelling on what we cannot change can only bring us anguish. **Studies show that hope is a critical factor in mental health**. An attitude of hope found in hostages makes a difference in survival. Hope is a great motivator and a source of mental and physical endurance. Most depression treatments work well in patients convinced that their mood can improve significantly and that they can be helped. Indeed, depression and anxiety often afflict those whose outlook on life is pessimistic, catastrophic, and hopeless. A hopeful attitude can make a big difference in our entire mental outlook.

Hopelessness impairs cognitive functioning. Hopelessness is defined as having no expectation of good or success, unable to be changed, and unable to be helped or improved. It is also the inability to learn, act, or perform. Synonyms for hopeless include words, such as despair, resignation, pointless, and impossible. When people feel uncertain, lost, and troubled in their careers and lives—sometimes, all they want is a good dosage of hope. Much like happiness, hope is an emotion that requires the individual to make good choices in order to sustain their positive impact. As such, the workplace culture can influence one's degree of happiness and hope. **Hope promotes mindfulness.** Mindfulness is living in a state of full conscious awareness of one's whole self, other people, and the context in which we live and work. Mindfulness engages our passion and builds on positive emotional states. Many individuals just want a leader to tell them that everything is going to be okay. They want a sense of security; a feeling that their worries will soon be gone. People search for hope to recapture that moment in time when they had minimal problems and felt their best.

Inspirational Leadership is about energizing and creating a sense of direction and purpose for followers, and excitement and momentum to achieve goals. Inspirational leaders are capable of taking an organization and people to new heights. How you are able to inspire your team through your own actions and examples is an important component in achieving leadership success. In her Harvard Business Review blog titled, *Hope Is a Strategy (Well, Sort Of)*, Deborah Mills-Scofield clearly articulates, "Hope is a critical part of achieving a strategy when based on what is possible; perhaps not highly probable, but possible. Hope is the belief that something is possible and probable, and the recognition that the degree of each is not necessarily equal. When hope is based on real-world experience, knowledge, and tangible and intangible data, it results in trust, which is necessary for implementing any strategy."

Hope influences positive social engagement and mental/physical well-being. Hope gives the belief, and opens the mind to finding solutions to problems; solutions you never thought existed. Research indicates that what really matters is that leaders are able to instil confidence, create enthusiasm, and be inspiring to the people they lead.Hope is a motivational force that causes people to stay focused and hang on. The fact is, no organization has ever become great without Inspirational Leadership as its cornerstone.

A leader's job is to help people believe that things will be fine, and they have the ability to make them okay. Great leaders cast a vision of hope; they instil a positive outlook toward days to come,and they give people something to look forward to—a better tomorrow and a brighter future. Giving hope to your people combines the alignment, engagement, and vision of the organization. A leader's ability to do so will reap enormous benefits for your organization and your people.Hope is telling your team that getting this challenging proposal done on time will open up new doors of business. The walls of your difficulty might seem too high to scale, but don't look up and don't look down. Look straight ahead; find that first base and start to climb. Soon, that wall will become merely a stepping stone to the next phase of your life—and your next adversity. Hope gives your people the drive to keep going in impending failure. Hope is reassuring the employees that their efforts will pay off and rough times will get better.

Please don't misunderstand; hope is not a good way to manage a business. Budgets, strategic plans, targets, and forecasts are all tools that leaders use to manage a business on a day to day basis, but hope is needed to lead people. Hope is intangible, but it is a matter of human nature that we all seek.

According to a Mercer consulting survey, one-third of U.S. employees are so unhappy that they are thinking of leaving their jobs. Zappos has achieved a reputation for superior customer service because it doesn't see employees as cogs in a wheel. Employees know that Zappos' leaders genuinely care about their well-being. It's also one of the "happiest" places in which to work...imagine that.

"A leader is a dealer in hope." —Napoleon Bonaparte

HOPE THEORY

Recent organizational research includes hope as a factor in human and social capital management. This is referred to as positive psychological capital (Luthans & Youssef). Luthans and Avolio (2003) recognize, "the force multiplier throughout history has often been attributed to the leader's ability to generate hope." Hope theory (Snyder, Irving & Anderson, 1991), developed within the field of positive psychology identifies hope as an activating force that enables people, even when faced with the most overwhelming obstacles, to envision a promising future and to set and pursue goals. It defines hope as a positive motivational state that is based on an interactively derived sense of successful (a)agencies (goal-directed energy), and (b) pathways (planning to meet goals), (Snyder, Irving & Anderson,). Hope is not just an emotion, it is a vibrant and potent force that contributes to leaders and followers expending the requisite energy necessary to pursue and attain organizational goals.

Shorey and Snyder (2004) describe hope as a cognitive goal-directed process composed of well-defined goals, the perceived ability to develop routes to those goals and possessing the requisite motivation. According to Snyder, Lopez, Shorey, Rand, and Feldman (2003), hope reflects individuals' perceptions regarding their capabilities to (a) clearly conceptualize goals, (b) develop the specific strategy to reach those goals (pathways thinking), and (c) initiate and sustain the motivation for using those strategies (agency thinking). Snyder (1994) pointed out that "high versus low-hope persons approach their life goals differently. Snyder stated **people with high hope** approach their goals with a focus on succeeding, have a positive emotional state and have a perception of a high probability of goal attainment. By contrast, **people with low hope** approach the achievement of their goals with a focus on failing rather than succeeding, have a negative emotional state and have a perception of low probability of goal attainment. Hoping can be seen as a deeply creative process; that allows the future to be shaped into possibility.

Shorey and Shorey (2004) argue that hope is a common process in leadership models, and explain how leaders can instil hope in their followers by having high expectations, considering followers needs and interests and maintaining a positive, affirming attitude toward followers. These actions and attitudes of leaders have positive effects on followers, namely resulting in trust and self-efficacy. Effective leadership, it would seem, awakens hopeful thinking. Cerff (2006) supports the role of hope as a future orientation, and notes the value of the inclusion of hope as an integral part of leadership development.

THREE BENEFITS OF HOPE

HOPE RESTORES FAITH

Faith is a deep-rooted assurance that affects the entire person. Faith is a principle that governs life. Faith is the means by which we reach out and grab on to a belief. Hope resets your belief system. Just as we cannot be fully human without love, we cannot be what we are intended to be without faith. Faith will increase if, when brought in contact with doubts and obstacles, we press on ahead regardless of how despondent the circumstances might be. Faith is more than a feeling; it's a principle that transcends the fickleness of human emotions.

As I left the corporate world and transitioned into the world of entrepreneurship, my journey was filled with many obstacles, disappointments and setbacks. There were many personal struggles. My leap of faith was against conventional wisdom. I left a lucrative position in the banking industry to start my own leadership consulting firm. Often times, I had to re-evaluate my friends as many of them either didn't understand or wasn't supportive of what I was trying to accomplish. It was difficult. I needed hope to get me through each day. Thankfully, my relationship with God, my mother, and my family would give me a sense of peace to plunge deeper and the focus to keep pursing my goals. Facing failures and the naysayers makes you more aware and allows you to use critical thinking/reasoning toward a longer-term solution.

Hope builds our self-confidence and inspires us to believe that we are capable of achieving great things by enabling us to aim higher and work smarter. Self-confidence becomes a platform in order to accept fresh thinking, and it motivates us to make new choices in our careers and life. Hope recalibrates your mind-set and makes you believe that there is a way out of your deepest fears. Cerff (2006) points out that hope "changes the way individuals view themselves, affects what individuals do with their lives, and provides power to live courageously and to be all that God intends them to be."

HOPE PROMOTES CLARITY

Hope broadens our observations and gives us the circular vision to see the goals we seek. Hope allows us to translate complexity into clarity; we begin to see through a broader lens. Hope fuels our perspective and energizes our fervent pursuits of endless possibilities. Hope gives us purpose and strengthens our will. Hope propels you during difficult times, and infuses you with happiness and keeps you moving toward your dreams, goals, and aspirations.

"A positive mind finds a way it can be done while a negative mind looks for all the ways it can't be done."—Napoleon Hill

Hope is the ultimate game changer that promotes the clarity and empowerment that we all need to move forward with our careers and lives. Every leader must have hope because without it, you become sceptical. According to a study featured in U.K.'s Daily Express, 63 percent of workers feel so depressed with their current career choice that they look on in envy at family and friends who seemingly have more productive and rewarding jobs.

HOPE HELPS TO INCREASE PRODUCTIVITY

Hope allows you to be more resourceful with your time, and gives you the energy you need for your daily work goals. We now become much more mindful about doing the right thing, and we are more focused in associating ourselves with the right people. Hope gives us the right attitude to keep pushing when circumstances say quit. Hope is a powerful force that brings people together. It instils a sense of unity, collective pride, and it strengthens optimism when people work together as one. This is why teambuilding is so powerful.

Two men are in prison. The gaze of one is drawn to the shiny, twinkling stars that bejewel the velvety firmament. As he takes in the beauty of this scene, he is filled with optimism and hope: there is something better beyond the bars! The other person focuses on the muddy ground surrounding the prison cells;nothing there encourages him, and he becomes less and less optimistic. He is robbed of hope because of the direction of his gaze.

7 WAYS LEADERS CAN INSTIL HOPE:

1 **Be visible**. Walk around the office. Be seen. Leaders must be present. They must show up. You are a symbol of hope. Let your body language and communication exude positivity.

2 **Be as open, honest,and as fair as possible**. Keep people in the picture. You must display authenticity if you want people to believe and trust you. Be realistic, but remain positive and hopeful for the future.

3 **Emphasize Optimism.** Former Secretary of State, Colin Powell, once said, "Optimism is a force multiplier." He also said that optimism was the "secret" behind President Ronald Reagan's charisma. Optimism is related to hope, but it is conceptually distinct from hope. Optimism involves the perceived ability to move toward goals with valued outcomes, and to avoid those that are undesirable, (Carver &Schemer, 1999). Hope enables us to be optimistic even in troubled circumstances. Optimism and hope often are crowded out of our lives by our busy schedules. It important to always emphasize; although we cannot change our external circumstances, we can change our attitude toward them.

4 **Encourage and Motivate**. The ability to instil hope in others requires that you truly care about the people involved and in the work they are doing. Engage and invite participation. Don't be over-critical. Followers must believe that their leaders believe in them, and that they will support them in their work and learning. Speak from the heart. I always tell my team how great they are, and encourage them to develop the endless possibilities that I see in each of them. Hope-driven leaders create environments where people flourish both personally and professionally.

5. **Focus on Possibility.** In John F. Kennedy's "We choose to go to the moon speech", He simply focused on possibility. We feel hope when we connect with that part of ourselves that wants to turn the impossible into reality.

6. **Let your people know how much you Value them**. This can be done through positive feedback, and rewards and recognition. If people feel they are valued, you will have their loyalty and support. "*People* work for money, but *go* the *extra mile* for recognition, praise, and rewards." —*Dale Carnegie*. Keep an eye on your peoples' health and wellbeing. Show that you care about their welfare and are interested in them.

7. **Invest in People.** Ensure that you have good training and development programmes. Ensure that they have the tools and the authority to do their work. Coaching and mentoring also foster self-reliance and self-worth, which are important factors when it comes to keeping motivation high.

Leaders also generate hope externally by the causes they support both locally and internationally. Companies do not function in isolation from the society around them. Philanthropic initiatives can also improve the local quality of life, which benefits all residents. Philanthropic social responsibility is all about a company caring about the world in which it exists and striving to improve that world for future generations;it involves making an effort to benefit society. This should be managed just as any other business activity; thus, it should be integrated into the daily operations. Make it part of your culture. Most importantly, it must be based on a genuine concern for people and the community. Show that you genuinely care and want to make a positive impact. Through *philanthropic* programs, leaders can bring much needed hope.

In 1996, S.C. Johnson, a manufacturer of cleaning and home-storage products, launched "Sustainable Racine", a project to make its home city in Wisconsin a better place in which to live and work. In partnership with local organizations, government, and residents, the company created a community-wide coalition focused on enhancing the local economy and the environment.

Pfizer developed a cost-effective treatment for the prevention of trachoma; the leading cause of preventable blindness in developing countries. In addition to donating the drugs, Pfizer worked with the Edna McConnell Clark Foundation, and world health organization to create the infrastructure needed to prescribe and distribute them to populations that previously had little access to healthcare; much less modern pharmaceuticals. Within one year, the incidence of trachoma was reduced by 50% among target populations in Morocco and Tanzania.

When you have the power to help others, do not ignore it. Sometimes, you may never know the impact you have made on others' lives, so never underestimate the depth of your influence.

A couple of months back, I met one of my previous employees Joanne in the supermarket. She was accompanied by her mother. Her mother was so happy to meet me because she said her daughter spoke highly of me. We chatted for a moment, then Joanne, thanking me, said "I can never forget the story you told about the Chinese bamboo. It still gives me hope." We parted ways and I went back to shopping. Then, as I was about to leave, Joanne hustled across and said "Brigette, I can still hear your voice in my head telling me "don't give up." I was blown away. I never knew my words had such a lasting impact on her. And, if she had never gotten the opportunity to tell me, I would have never known.

This is the story that I had shared with my team about the Chinese bamboo. You can take a Chinese bamboo seed, and then plant and nurture it for four years without visibly seeing any growth except for a tiny sprout. During that period, all the growth was underground, spreading a massive root structure. But then, in the fifth year, it produces 90 feet of growth in six short weeks. You can literally watch the plant grow. Your goals in life can be likened to the Chinese Bamboo tree. Sometimes you work hard, but don't see any growth for weeks, months, or even years; there seems to be no fruit for all your effort and energy expended. But, if you keep working and believing, one day your seeds will suddenly germinate. All it takes is a little patience and faith and you yourself, will be blown away at the extent of growth taking place.

Hope is a vital component of a leader's life. The leaders' hope surrounds the belief that his goal will be attained. It enables one to face tough times with creativity and resilience. Leading in these uncertain times requires inspiration more than ever. The ability to instil hope is a necessary leadership trait. However, one of the most important things that a leader must do is provide clarity of direction. As a leader, you are first and foremost judged on the results that you deliver. While in organizations, hope without a good business strategy is most certainly a recipe for disaster; the opposite is equally as true. Hope can certainly be a viable strategy—but without substance, value, and daily progress, selling hope becomes limited and irresponsible. Don't abuse the power of hope. Don't give people unfounded or false hope. Only use hope as a means if you can truly help people move in a more positive direction.

CHAPTER TWO

HUMILITY: The Foundation of All Great Leaders

Mirror, mirror on the wall;who is really the best and the brightest of all?

Who doesn't aspire to *be great*? In reality, who in their right mind would rather be the one serving rather than being served? Is it not the whole point of life to get ahead, to become influential; someone who is waited on and attended to by others? Many people associate humility with being weak or ineffective, and most don't admire others for being humble. Humility seems very much lost in our self-centred culture, and narcissistic, ego-driven leaders have become the norm.

The average Fortune 500 CEO makes $10-$15 million per year, is surrounded by immense executive perks, and has hundreds of employees under their control. However, despite their lavish perks and pay, the average Fortune 500 CEO lasts less than five years. In his 2005 *Harvard Business Review* article, author Jim Collins postulated a higher level of leader characterized by humility and a fierce resolve. He stated that "The *X-Factor* of great leadership is not personality; it's *humility.*"

Humility is an incredibly powerful choice. Humility is the gateway for other traits, such as empathy, authenticity, and integrity. Humble leaders are great listeners and welcome feedback. "With pride comes disgrace, but with humility comes wisdom" (Proverbs 11:2). When we look at some of the world's greatest leaders whose influence seems to have strengthened in their absence, humility is one common trait they embodied. Scientific inquiry into the power and effectiveness of humility has shown that it offers a significant "competitive advantage" to leaders.

According to a study from the University of Washington Foster School of Business, humble people tend to make *the most* effective leaders and are more likely to be high performers in both individual and team settings, according to associate professor, Michael Johnson. "Our study suggests that a 'quieter' leadership approach -- listening, being transparent, aware of your limitations, and appreciating co-workers strengths and contributions, is an effective way to engage employees," Johnson, and fellow researchers, Bradley Owens, and Terence Mitchell, write in the study.

Jewish Rabbi, Nilton Bonder, explained it beautifully when he said, "Many people believe that humility is the opposite of pride when; in fact, it is a point of equilibrium. The opposite of pride is actually a lack of self-esteem. A humble person is totally different from a person who cannot recognize and appreciate himself as part of this world's marvels."

"Humility is a strange thing; the minute you think you've got it, you've lost it" —Sir *Edward* Hulse. A small city wanted to identify and reward its meekest resident. A survey was taken, which ultimately identified the person. In a ceremony attended by all the dignitaries, the meekest person was presented with a medal on which were engraved the words, "The Meekest Man in Town." However, the next day, they had to take the medal away from him because he kept wearing it and showing it off!

Alexander, Julius Caesar, Napoleon, and Genghis Khan, amongst others, all saw leadership in terms of power and authority over others. Humility has such a delicate nature that it can't be faked for long.

"Sense shines with a double lustre when it is set in humility. An able, and yet humble man is a jewel worth a kingdom." —William Penn

HOW TO SPOT HUMILITY IN LEADERS

1. **Is their vocabulary mainly comprised of "I" rather than of "we" and "us?"** Do they put the interests of the team before theirs? Humble leaders **consistently seek opportunities to help and to serve others.** Humility arises out of strength, not weakness. To be humble, one needs confidence and self-restraint. Humility is the ceasing to fight for your own agenda, but rather that of the multitude. The humble leader is not occupied with self. The humble person is one who has learnt to control self, which takes true strength. Many leaders mistake controlling, dominating, or other harsh behaviours for strength. Humility takes strength and is the opposite of pride and arrogance; it is the mastery

of self-leadership. This is not to suggest that humble leaders are soft or unwilling to make tough decisions; they do so not for themselves, but for the greater good of their organizations. Humility develops from an inner sense of self-worth. Humble leaders are grounded by the principles by which they lead. Ultimately, they know that to lead is to serve others being their customers, employees, stakeholders, communities, etc. It requires acts of courage, such as taking personal risks for the greater good.

"True humility is not thinking less of yourself; it is thinking of yourself less." —C.S. Lewis

2 Are they boastful? Do they take all the credit for success? Humility promotes self-reflection and self-awareness, as you are able to honestly assess your own strengths and weaknesses. Being honest about the skills you possess and the value you can bring to clients and a company is the best way to avoid getting in over your head. Humility helps to keep us grounded and appreciative of what we have, and it helps us to see that there is a greater need than our own selfish desires. Humble leaders do not take advantage of their positional power. To be a great developer of people, you must be personally secure because taking your people to the height of their potential may mean they may pass you by. Fulfilment doesn't come from power, but through service. Leaders obtain influence not via position, but servanthood. They are not defined by their achievements (good or bad), and can easily separate who they are from what they do. When their accomplishments attract praise, they are quick to

acknowledge the contribution of others and easily give them credit. Additionally, they don't shift the blame when they fail. Proud leaders seem to have all the right answers; humble leaders seem to have all the right questions. Humility means being open to the fact that I don't know everything, and that I can learn something from everyone.

3 How do they handle criticism or opposition? Are they open to other people's perspectives? How do they speak about others or competitors? Narcissistic leaders take things personally and may speak without careful consideration. Humble leaders are able to accept expert input that may or may not agree with their own thoughts, and make good decisions based on all of the inputs, not just those that confirm to their own bias. They are able to abandon their pet plans in favour of superior alternatives. Humble people recognize boundaries and respect others. Everyone takes notice of how praise and blame are handed out. Make sure your feedback doesn't demean anyone. Humility promotes an environment that values empathy. Listen while receiving feedback and have respect for others. Humility is manifested in how we relate to others. It is revealed in words, attitudes, and actions. To be humble means to manifest humility. Humble leaders reward in public, and discipline in private.

4 **How do you feel when you are around them?** Insignificant, great, empowered? If you can strip away the surface of pride, you show a human side. Humble leaders are not afraid to show their vulnerability, which makes them more human and approachable. Leaders are difficult to be around if they *always* have to be the smartest person in the room. That's important because people want to work with, and work for, leaders they like. People should be straightforward with you; they should not be afraid of you. *Draw people by your humility* and honour, not by your position and power. Humble leaders look at others as equals, not as subordinates. Humble people allow others to assert themselves because they are already assertive. Humility reminds us that it's not about us, and it reminds us to focus on what really matters. Leaders put empathy ahead of authority. Such leaders are friendly, and not arrogant or egotistical. *Humble leaders look at others as equals, not as subordinates.* They don't allow their position of authority to make them feel that they're better than anyone else. We gravitate to such leaders because they make everyone that they come in contact with feel valued no matter their level from the janitor to the Chairman of the Board. In difficult times, people rely on humble leaders even more to get them through crises.

5. **Do they admit when they are wrong?** Humility is being able to admit that you were wrong. Leaders are teachable. Leaders are continuous learners who are always willing to learn new things. If you can't admit you're wrong, you can't grow. Leaders must be willing to say when they are wrong and admit their mistakes. Humble leaders are great listeners and usually possess high Emotional Intelligence. *They are not afraid to show their vulnerability, which makes them more human and easier to relate to.* An apology is the sign of a strong leader. Great leaders are aware of their own

imperfections, so they **forgive others'** mistakes. They offer grace to those that have offended them. Humility doesn't mean a lack of confidence. Great leaders need to care about and respect those around them no matter their level; they should possess the ability to offer grace to those that have offended them. They also need to be able to see themselves for who they are and be completely comfortable with it.

"The first to apologize is the bravest. The first to forgive is the strongest. And, the first to forget is the happiest." —Unknown

6 **Do they take themselves too seriously?** Humour opens the mind to learn from others. Humble leaders are strong, but light-hearted. This helps promote an upbeat atmosphere. They can laugh at themselves and can see the humour in situations, which helps to put everyone at ease. Humour is a great way to win over and influence a team. It minimizes status distinctions between leaders and followers, and encourages interaction. The humble leader will use self-critical humour whereas the arrogant leader will focus their humour on others. Self-critical humour tends to minimize status distinctions between leaders and employees. More specifically, the attributes of self-critical humour should include having an honest and humble view of one's self and an appreciation and respect of others. Leaders who use humour allow people to feel comfortable around them. It is humanizing and puts others at ease. Leaders who use humour tend to be much more approachable than the person who never laughs. The more approachable you are, especially as a leader, the more comfortable people will feel around you. Humour acts as a catalyst to influence and inspire others. It helps foster an upbeat atmosphere that encourages interaction, engagement, brainstorming, and creative thinking. All of which leads to greater productivity.

7 **Do they embrace succession planning?** Humble leaders share their knowledge and enjoy watching their followers grow and develop? Business scholar, James Collins, and a research team, conducted a five year historical analysis of companies that over time had made a sustained transition from good to great. Succession planning was a problem. Collins writes, "In over three quarters of the comparison companies, we found that executives **set their successors up for failure,** chose weak successors, or both."

"We rise by lifting others." —Robert Ingersoll

THE IMPORTANCE OF HUMILITY

Humility is an essential quality for authentic leaders. People trust them because they know they are genuine and honest. Lacking those qualities in leaders leads to distrust and fear. When we teach people to be afraid, they are being held captive. Narcissist leaders want complete control of everything and lead by fear. Such leaders control others by unambiguity; they don't disclose information or reveal the truth.

Humility is a virtue, but on the other hand, can you have *too much* of it? *Some argue that too much humility can be a bad thing.* If one has a root of humility firmly planted, it's not something you can turn off or on, it's a natural overflow of a sincere heart. The 12th century philosopher, Maimonides, believed that the "middle way" was the best way to live. Humility must not be confused with shyness or allowing others to trample all over you. Developing humility is a process to a higher consciousness. Humility can help you become a more effective leader. Humility serves as an antidote to protect us from the poisonous effects of an unrestrained ego, it dispels harmful pride, and negates the self-absorption of narcissism. Arrogance will betray an immaturity to power. The ego loves praise, clouds your judgement, and blinds us with a false sense of invincibility; thus, leading to poor decisions and a breakdown of relationships. Humility, on the other hand, allows one to set their ego aside. When consistently pursued and prudently polished over time, it is a powerful force for good that helps to sustain success, and also, draws people to us. If one has a root of humility firmly planted, it's not something you can turn off or on, it's a natural overflow of a pure, sincere heart.

CHAPTER THREE

Authenticity: The Gold Standard of Leadership

"All the world's a stage, and all the men and women merely players: they have their exits and their entrances, and one man in his time plays many parts; his acts being seven ages." — William Shakespeare

There is a great line from the movie, *Into the Woods,* spoken by Prince Charming, "Hey, my mother raised me to be charming, not sincere." And, that is how some of us choose to live our lives. Leadership is about authenticity. Learning to be true to yourself can be difficult. We are all bombarded by so many external voices pressuring us on whom we should be and how we should act. Everyday leaders are closely scrutinized for their words and their actions, as they become role models for people inside and outside of their organizations. Leaders ask us to follow, to sacrifice, and to believe.

On September 17th, 2004, the renowned theologian Jürgen Moltmann gave a presentation before Yale University theology faculty entitled, "Control is Good but Trust is Better." True Leaders lead by influence which requires trust. Therefore for us to trust a leader, their leadership must be genuine. It must be a true reflection of their strengths, weakness, values, and culture.

7 SIGNS OF AUTHENTICITY IN LEADERS

- ➲ **Authentic leadership starts with Self-Awareness**. Authenticity in leadership begins when one truly understands who they are and how they impact their environment. It's important to develop a leadership style that is consistent with your character and personality. Authenticity requires one to become aware of their deep subconscious intentions and motives. One learns to maximize their strengths and work on their weaknesses. Self-aware leaders go to great lengths to learn from their mistakes and errors. What matters most is to be yourself. So, being genuinely authentic no matter what the context is a real test of how well you know and are comfortable with being yourself. People should have a regular process for self-examination because this is key to becoming self-aware. Reflection leads to self-awareness.

Self-Awareness Leads to Insight

Self-Aware leaders should ask themselves the following questions if they want to maximize their leadership skills and effectiveness.

- What drives me?
- What do I really want?
- What do I believe in?
- How am I impacting others?
- Do I put my agenda first or those of others?
- Am I being truthful? What areas do I need to work on to be absolutely sincere?

Authentic Leaders engage in reflection and introspective practices. You need to figure out your underlying passions and motivations to ultimately discover your purpose. When you know your purpose, you have greater resiliency and courage to stick with what's right versus what others expect of you.

"Authenticity has become the gold standard for leadership" —Harvard Business Review

Over the past few decades, psychologists have given a revealing survey to more than 23,000 people at work. Here are some of the assertions:

- My behaviour is usually an expression of my true inner feelings, attitudes, and beliefs
- I would not change my opinions (or the way I do things) in order to please someone else or win their favour
- I'm always the person I appear to be

People who answer true are perceived as highly authentic—they know and express their genuine selves. And, a rigorous analysis of all 136 studies shows that these authentic people receive significantly *lower* performance evaluations and are significantly *less likely* to get promoted into leadership roles.

When people feel like they can be themselves, express themselves, and be true to themselves at work, they ultimately feel happier. A study from the Harvard Business Review found that happiness at work raises nearly every business outcome including increasing sales by 37 percent, and productivity by 31 percent. When people can be themselves and speak their mind, they bring different perspectives, which fuels better innovation and problem solving, which just makes good business sense. Employee engagement has also reached a low point. In a worldwide Gallup poll,only 13% of employees were engaged at work, and the greatest reason for changing jobs was a result of mistrust, misalignment of values, frustration, and burnout.

⮑ **Authentic leaders are genuine**. To **quote** *Hamlet:* **"To thine own self be true."** Those who always try "to be the right person in the right place at the right time," according to Mark Snyder, a social psychologist at the University of Minnesota, become extraordinarily attuned to the ways that others react to them. They continually monitor their social performance, skilfully adjusting it when they detect that they are not having the desired effect. However, people can spot a "phony" a mile away. We live in a world where society has adopted an acceptability of false perceptions. The focus is mostly on selling and promoting a false version of us, and by learning at a very young age to simply fake it. Some of us are conditioned throughout life to just fit in and we will do whatever it takes.

"To find your own true authentic leadership voice amid all the clutter of the noise is one of the great challenges of your life."—Nares Nirumvala

⮑ **Authenticity takes courage.** Authentic leadership is daring to be different and real. If you try to be something you're not, others will know it and so will you; you can't fake it. Who you really are is embedded naturally within you. Some leaders may pull it off for a while, but eventually, the truth comes to light. Lack of authenticity is revealed in both body language and impromptu comments in unguarded moments. Many business leaders and politicians have been driven to become chameleons to cover their vulnerabilities. The negative impact of wearing a mask is that others can sense that something is not quite right. They get a gut feeling of uncertainty as to whether the person is being genuine. Trust and authenticity are intricately woven together. When people feel uncertain about you, they will most likely distrust you. If they distrust you, they will not respect you as a leader. Authentic leaders are transparent. You would be better able to inspire people if they have an intuitive good feeling about you. True effective leadership requires authenticity and trust. It leads to success through employee commitment and engagement. These are the initial building blocks to great organizations.

➲ **They are individuals of integrity.** To live authentically, you must ensure that your actions align with your beliefs and principles. Authenticity and integrity go hand in hand. Integrity is where your beliefs, convictions, thoughts, and behaviours are integrated together in your life. A person of integrity purposely follows a moral code. A major element in anyone's completeness as a person is following the set of values in which you believe in and by which you strive to live. Researchers from Columbia, Northwestern, and Harvard worked together to scientifically measure authenticity. They found that when people failed to behave authentically, they experienced an intensified state of discomfort that is usually associated with immorality. People who weren't true to themselves were so disturbed that they felt a strong need to cleanse themselves physically. Our brains know when we're living a lie and, like all untruths, being inauthentic causes harm.

➲ **Authentic leaders are confident.** Authenticity means stepping out of your comfort zone and taking risks. When you are comfortable living in your own skin by your values, you will be much more prepared to stand up for those values when the time comes. You will have the courage to lead, guide, and inspire others in what you believe to be true and honest. It's about integrity. Much social anxiety originates from the fear of being found out; someone may remove the mask. People who are not genuine are afraid that somebody is going to discover that they're not as smart, qualified, or established as they pretend to be. Authentic people don't have that fear. Authentic leaders can be themselves without pretence because they have nothing to prove to anyone except themselves because they are confident in their own skin. They can openly acknowledge that they don't know everything. They know how to ask others for help. They have confidence in their own strengths and weakness, and acknowledge that these exist. *Authentic leaders are not perfect, nor do they try to be.* They make mistakes, but they are willing to admit and learn from them. They are truthful, honest, and open, and they inspire their employees to higher commitments and extraordinary efforts. It is no wonder that companies are now focusing on the importance of this trait. This confidence comes from the fact that they have nothing to hide. Who they appear to be is who they really are. Leaders need to be true to themselves and to others. It takes courage to look inside and be what you need to be.

⮑ **They establish connected relationships**. Authentic leaders genuinely care about people and empower people to lead. If you pretend to care about other people, they won't respond much to your interest. If you actually care, they will open up to you. Such leaders seek honest feed back about themselves and their leadership. They honour others openly. They sincerely empathize with others. By showing empathy, leaders can see the world through another's eyes. This helps to build an open and transparent culture. Authentic leaders are humble leaders; they talk less and listen more. Listening gives leaders the opportunity to connect with people on a completely new level by building stronger and more trusted relationships. *Authentic leadership facilitates mutual value between leader and follower.* Your values define your working relationships. As a leader, you need to hold the bar even higher, and set the standard for others to follow. Your business and its employees reflect your values.

⇒ **They have a unique brand.** Each of us should strive to be the best version of ourselves. To discover and accept who we truly are is a life-long journey. Everyone has a personal brand, but many of us are not aware of it. In fact, personal branding is deeply rooted in our search for identity and meaning in life; it's the message that we constantly share about ourselves. Personal branding is strongly rooted in our uniqueness, and it reflects our authenticity, values, and strengths. Wouldn't it be preferable for people to focus on reputation rather than brand? After all, you can buy yourself a brand, butyou have to build your reputation. This uniqueness is not falsely fabricated, but it truly emanates from ourselves. This is about naturally influencing others by embracing our uniqueness, and we all know that uniqueness attracts people and opportunities. In other words, being yourself starts by unconditionally loving yourself and others.

"Be yourself; everyone else is already taken." —Oscar Wilde

IS "BE YOURSELF" TERRIBLE ADVICE FOR A LEADER?

The concept of authenticity means many different things to different people. It basically is not putting on a show and being true to yourself. The practice of authenticity is liberating and growth-inducing but in reality, it can also mean remaining as I have always been. The problem with authenticity is that if you have a one-dimensional view of it, you may be impeding your growth.Leaders may latch on to authenticity as an excuse for sticking with what's comfortable. Being authentic is not an excuse for ignoring personal development. If a leader says "I don't like to listen to people, so I am being authentic when I don't",that would be rather silly. Your image matters, especially when you're in a business environment. For example, if you are going to a business lunch, you should follow the protocols of business dining etiquette. This is wisdom.The problem is that what feels like the authentic *you* is really the old self that you need to let go of in order to be a better leader. In reality, nearly anything that gets us out of our comfort zone, such as any new leadership behaviour, will feel artificial at first.Inexperienced leaders often find the process of getting buy-in distasteful and inauthentic because it feels synthetic. Authentic leaders search for wisdom. They do not burst out with whatever they may be feeling. Rather, they exhibit self-monitoring and use emotional intelligence to communicate effectively. Authenticity doesn't require that a leader bares their soul and gives details of all their vulnerabilities and insecurities. Researchers have suggested that people who want to be seen authentically are more likely to share information that jeopardizes their professional relationships. Authenticity needs to be tempered and examined if we're to grow and develop in the ways we long for.There must be a balance, and that is where wisdom comes in. Becoming authentic is a developmental state that enables leaders to progress through multiple roles as they learn and grow from their experiences.

CAN TRUST BE REBUILT?

Can confidence be regained once it is lost through the lack of authenticity? Trust is nearly impossible to regain in any relationship once it's lost.It depends on the extent of the damage and if people are willing to overlook it. It can be rebuilt, but regaining trust is a process. The leader has to own their mistakes and show they are taking the necessary steps to improve themselves. It will definitely take a lot of work and effort. Don't expect it to happen overnight. Personal accountability backed with consistent and truthful actions are critical. You will have to constantly prove yourself. Trust can only be restored over time;however, it may not be at the original extent it was at. There may be some doubt by those who have experienced the inauthentic behaviour, but with time, people do forgive.

If you want your team to trust you and you want their commitment, you will need to be authentic. Living authentically is a noble path that you won't regret following. Authentic leadership is a constant journey and commitment, both to your own growth and to the growth of others.

CHAPTER FOUR

INTEGRITY & HONESTY At Work: Building Trust

Integrity is one of the top attributes of a great leader. Research on leadership has consistently rated integrity as one of the most important character traits of a respected leader. Integrity, defined as "Adherence to moral and ethical principles, soundness of moral character; honesty; a state of being whole, entire, or undiminished." It's an alignment between a person's values, beliefs, words and actions. It connotes a deep commitment to do the right thing for the right reasons. It is at the core of who you are as a person. It builds trust. Everything boils down to this—if your team can't trust you, vendors don't believe you, and customers will not support your business. Who would you rather follow: someone who is honest, consistent in their high character, and trustworthy? Or someone who isn't?

Trusting someone takes a lot of faith and belief in them. Jean Francois Gravelet, better known as The Great Blondin, became famous for walking across Niagara Falls on a tightrope. In September of 1860, the Prince of Wales had witnessed Blondin's crossing of the falls with an assistant on his back. After making it across, Blondin turned to the British prince and offered to carry him across the falls too. Although the prince had heard of his skills, and had just *witnessed him* in action, he was still not ready to place his life in Blondin's hands.

Abraham Lincoln, the best known U.S. president for having integrity, once said: "Great leadership is a product of great character. And, that is why character matters." When the Watergate scandal in the United States was exposed by the press in the early 1970's, it was revealed that much of the White House activity focused on cover-up operations. When President Richard Nixon finally resigned, it was not because he either had authorized the break-in to the Democratic Party's premises or had a part in planning the break-in; instead, he was guilty of trying to cover up what others had done.

The decisions and choices we make behind closed doors when no one is looking define the fabric of our character. Your moral compass should be able to distinguish right from wrong and good from evil. Zig Ziglar says *"With integrity, you have nothing to fear since you have nothing to hide. With integrity, you will do the right thing, so you will have no guilt."* Leaders today have to live in glass houses and be transparent and accountable for everything they say and do. So, honesty and integrity have become qualities that are vital for survival.

Frenchman Jean Jacques Rousseau (1712-1778), sometimes deemed the philosopher of the French Revolution, argued that "there is no original sin in the human heart" and that human beings are all basically good. It was society, he said, that had corrupted humanity. If left to our own devices, to our own feelings and conscience, we would naturally do the right thing (all this from a man who, after fathering a number of children, dumped them all at an orphanage).

In 2012, trust in business leaders fell to an all-time low (Edelman Trust Barometer.) A lack of authenticity and transparency, led to a huge mistrust of many financial institutions following the financial crisis. We've witnessed integrity's downfall over the last 20 or so years in almost every area of culture. Corporate scandals have rocked the business world. Bernard Madoff was found to be an investment fraud artist. As well, the collapse of the U.S.based Enron Corp., a leader in energy, is embedded in our memories. The leadership at Enron was found to have engaged in accounting fraud and corruption, which was abetted by the Arthur Anderson accounting firm. Both went bankrupt while key leaders faced prison terms. Scandals among politicians and celebrities dominate headlines. As a result, we have grown increasingly cynical. Whether a single lapse of integrity and/or as a continuous way of doing business, unethical leadership behaviour has the power to ruin a career and to totally destroy an organization. When integrity is destroyed, confidence is lost and may never return. Such leaders leave a trail of destruction and many people hurt are hurt in the process. At Enron 20,000 staff suddenly lost their jobs through no fault of their own.

James Kouzes and Barry Posner describe their survey of over 75,000 employees around the world. They found that "honesty" in leaders (which aligns directly with integrity) was selected more than any other characteristic as desirable in a leader. It seems employees think integrity is important.

Leaders with integrity inspire confidence in others. In business, **integrity is an absolute must**. A lot of business leaders don't even realize how closely they're being watched by their subordinates. Your ability to influence is not just based on skill or intelligence; it's based in trust and requires integrity, which is the foundation of real and lasting influence. Unethical behaviour does not occur in a vacuum. Many people in the company know. The issue will not go away; it will only get worse, and is a latent legal, financial, and reputation risk. There are two critical components of integrity. The first is the adherence to anethical principle. This isn't simply compliance to a law or a rule; it implies an understanding of the reason it exists. The second is the pursuit of an established standard. No one is perfect; we all make mistakes, but those with integrity admit their mistakes and consistently move toward doing the right things.

The word 'character' is derived from the Greek word *charattein*, meaning to engrave. This provides a much clearer understanding of integrity as something we can grow and develop. The German proverb **"Einmal ist Keinmal."** Means "once doesn't count." It's an idiomatic expression for the idea that if something happens only once, it might as well have never happened at all. Every time you do the right thing, you become stronger.

Much effort had gone into the preparation that eventually led to Roger Bannister running the mile in under four minutes. There was endless training and practice. Meanwhile, others around the world were training for the same prize which meant so much to this young athlete. May 6, 1954 dawned; the day that Roger Bannister had been preparing for emotionally, spiritually, mentally and physically for years. Yet, the morning before—he had slipped on a polished floor and hobbled the rest of that day! Nevertheless, the race began the next day, and Roger Bannister ran the mile in three minutes, 59.4 seconds—the first person to run the mile in less than four minutes. Someone once asked an award-winning, long-distance runner if the runner thought this person could become a great runner as well. "Sure," the athlete replied, "all you need to do is run 15 miles a day for six days a week, and then on the seventh, run 25. Do that for a year and you'll have a good chance of making it." Using imagery from athletics, integrity is like training for a long distance race. Over time, you will develop endurance and, if you slip, get back and keep doing the right thing. There are many things you can lack and still steer clear of danger; integrity isn't one of them.

Establish a set of sound ethics policies, integrate them into all business processes, communicate them broadly to all employees, and make clear that you will not tolerate any deviation from any of them. Then, live by them. —Michael Hyatt

Over the years, I've witnessed many brilliant leaders falling of the ladder because they were willing to cut corners by falsifying numbers on their results or embellishing their resume. I have also seen leaders crumble by the facades they present. When the pressure is on, the "real person" comes out. If you have integrity and are comfortable in your own skin, you won't need to deceive anyone.

"The supreme quality for leadership is unquestionably integrity. —Dwight D. Eisenhower

Don't cut corners or sacrifice quality. There are no shortcuts; they eventually lead to dead ends. In 2015, Forbes listed Elizabeth Holmes as the world's youngest self-made woman billionaire worth an estimated $4.5 billion. She founded Theranos; a blood-testing company in 2003. The company had developed blood analysis machines that could "automate and miniaturize more than 1,000 laboratory tests" in a manner that would "require only microscopic blood volumes." But, everything came tumbling when the truth came out and it was discovered that the company wasn't using its own blood analysis machines to do many of its tests, and that there were accuracy concerns over the tests that were done on its machines. Federal regulators banned Holmes from owning or operating a medical laboratory for at least two years, and that Theranos could no longer continue operating its California lab.Forbes recently announced that the *net worth* of *Elizabeth Holmes*, founder and CEO of Theranos, had fallen from $4.5 billion to $0.

Research from the Institute of Leadership and Management shows that while 83% of managers say their organizations have value statements, only 38% consider they are closely aligned to those statements. That's a huge disconnect. Further, some 63% of people surveyed believe they have been asked to take action that goes against the values of their business. Your vision and values should work in unison with each other much like the nervous system and the muscular system. But, for many people, that's not the case. *Often, their values are an afterthought.* Getting what we want, in and of itself, is not the problem. Our problem with integrity happens when we ask ourselves, "How can I get what I want?" Rather, the question should be "How can I get what I want and be the person I want to be?" The person we want to be is more important than the things we think we want to get.

In a 1995 survey, some athletes were asked the following question: If there was a drug you could take that would guarantee you'd receive a gold medal at the Olympics, but that would kill you in five years, would you take it? More than 50 percent said yes. It is an example of the appeal of fame and power on our society. To be "in front of the camera," and celebrated by millions, is what many people crave.

INTEGRITY MEANS:

- ➲ Leading by example. It can be likened to a parent/child relationship. You cannot set policies that employees need to live by and not live by them yourself

- ➲ Standing up for what is right

- ➲ Keeping your word. Be reliable. Keeping promises, meeting important deadlines, and being there when people need you

⊃ Expressing concern for the common good

⊃ Being honest when no one is looking

⊃ Doing the honourable thing even when it's not popular

⊃ Loyalty under temptation or duress

⊃ Never compromising on a principle even when encouraged to

⊃ Making fair decisions

⊃ Communicating honestly

⊃ Giving credit where it's due

⊃ Displaying consistency in your words and actions

⊃ Treating everyone with respect

Someone once asked a politician, "Have you kept all the promises that you made during the campaign?" He responded, "Yes . . . well, at least all the promises that I intended to keep."

We have all come across other leaders in the business that are great at displaying smoke and mirrors. Many times, the smoke and mirrors is simply a reflection of what management wants from them to grow the bottom-line. Acting with integrity as a leader means that you won't always be the most liked because doing the right thing isn't always the popular thing. Integrity is consistently behaving in a principled manner no matter who is watching. Consistency is an important concept in the framework of integrity. People need consistency. They need to know where they stand and what to expect. People want a leader who practices what he or she preaches and who follows through on promises. They must "walk the talk."

Integrity is something that is built over time, not overnight. Building integrity starts with the smallest act and moves forward from there; snowballing into a reputation of trustworthiness and honesty.

A young man purchased a pleasure boat with a nice little motor and trailer. The unit appeared in excellent condition, although it was not new and—it was not too expensive. Eager to try out his new acquisition, he invited some friends and took the boat out. It ran smoothly, and the group made their way to a small island off the mainland in Lake Ontario. Anchoring the little boat, they explored the island, and then returned to the boat to head home. A short distance out, a splashing sound alerted them to the fact that they were taking on water. Quickly, the boat capsized, throwing the three friends into the chilly waters. A most fortunate rescue prevented serious repercussions. What had happened? A single rotted timber was found in the base of the hull that, with the wave action on the beach, had led to a split in the wood. **Just one bad piece out of all the others was enough to overturn the boat.**

CORE VALUES!

Imagine that you at a service provider waiting to pay a bill. You stand in line for a long period and worry about missing a meeting. Finally, you are the next person in line. You go to the counter and pay the bill and leave. On your way out, you count your change and discover that you have been given way too much. What do you do? Return the money and perhaps miss your meeting or consider this your lucky day and move on? What you do in this situation will depend on your understanding of right and wrong. Ethics is the way that we apply this understanding in our everyday life. Today, the most popular type of ethics is **situational ethics**, which submit that there are no moral absolutes. It often means doing whatever is most beneficial for oneself in a particular situation.

Not practicing integrity is similar to playing Russian roulette. In 1982, an unusual work of modern art went on display. It was a shotgun affixed to a chair. The artwork could be viewed by sitting in the chair and looking directly into the gun barrel. The problem was that the gun was loaded and set on a timer to fire at an undetermined moment within the next hundred years. Amazingly enough, people waited in lines to sit and stare into the shell's path, although they knew that the gun could go off at any moment. Talk about tempting fate! Unfortunately, people do the same thing with unethical practices, thinking that they can stare disaster in the face and still get away unharmed.

"There is no pillow so soft as a clear conscience." —Proverb

BE TRUTHFUL

In the words of Thomas Jefferson, a great thinker of his time, "Honesty is the first chapter in the book of Wisdom." Lying, in and of itself, is bad enough, but doing it in court and under oath is even worse. In many countries, perjury is a crime, and a serious one at that. The witness must therefore give a truthful testimony. Some people don't consider lying bad. In fact, it's not like you are killing anyone. Sadly though, if you are dishonest in small matters, you will be dishonest in large matters. It all starts as a small snowball, and turns into an avalanche before you yourself have realized how far you have gone.

It is better to remain contented or even to lose a promotion, if we have to lie in order to get it or if we have to sacrifice our integrity. Integrity is a lot easier to talk about than to display. Even the best of us find ourselves easily compromised unless we are careful. Truly, in the littlest things, it is so easy to slip. A couple of years ago, I missed out on a huge promotion because I didn't comply with an action from a CEO of my then establishment. He instructed me to hold back a delinquent customer's payment, so their mortgage would be transferred to the non-accrual status, so that his colleague could supposedly submit an offer to purchase this prime property.

Unfortunately, early in our life, we learned that dishonesty can have great short-term benefits. It can get us out of trouble and it can get us what we want. And, all of us develop the habit (albeit, to varying degrees). Philosopher Sissle Bok has convincingly demonstrated how lying can be harmful for society. She writes: A society then, whose members were unable to distinguish truthful messages from deceptive ones, would collapse. — *Lying: Moral Choice in Public and Private Life* (New York: Pantheon Books, 1978), p. 19. Likewise, St. Augustine, as quoted in the introduction of Bok's book, noted that when regard for truth has been broken down or even slightly weakened, all things will remain doubtful.

If you lead long enough, you will face moral dilemmas, but integrity must always be in the front of your mind. Honesty builds confidence and strengthens your character. Dishonesty can be stressful, as it needs to be maintained. When you have nothing to hide, you are at peace because you don't have to maintain false stories or a double life. Remember, character is built over time and in the small moments. The seemingly trivial decisions you make when no one is watching will carve your character.

The leader is the one who upholds and enables the development of a moral system in an organization. Healthy organizations have a strong sense of moral order. It doesn't mean they are perfect, but they know who they are, and what they are about. There are certain lines they don't dare cross.

Paul Polman, Unilever CEO, took the decision to eliminate quarterly profit reporting in order to for the business to focus on the longer-term. Consequently, Unilever's share price fell 8% as short-term investors pulled out. His action told employees that their leader won't compromise on matters of principle and it reassured them that he had their best interests at heart. What was the result? In the five years since that decision was taken, Unilever showed "consistent sales growth and margin expansion coupled with strong cash flow." As a result, its share price roughly doubled over the period.

Integrity is essential; therefore there must be accountability. Many people don't like to hear the truth. If it's negative, they see it as a personal attack on them. Is there someone in your life who can tell you when you are going on a wrong path and who will keep you in touch with reality? Society longs for leaders of integrity. To practice integrity means seeking out the best for your employees. This means that in your decisions, you set aside personal gain and put into consideration what would be beneficial to your people. Integrity entails that you become a "steward" of your people. You take care and become responsible for their well-being.

While most leaders don't engage in fraudulent behaviour, many walk in the "**grey area**." In other words, while they aren't engaging in anything illegal, their behaviour can be considered unethical. And, it only takes one small step to cross the line. Leaders want their companies to be profitable, but this should be done only within the confines of sound legal and ethical precepts. Ethical leaders function within both the **letter and the "spirit' of the law**. They are sensitive to the fact that their everyday business decisions may have deleterious effects on others. The financial crisis of 2007-08 revealed that there is a higher need for ethical leaders and transparency in business processes. Success without integrity really isn't success at all.

Integrity is the foundation of any good reputation. People will talk, and when they speak about you, it is best that you give them nothing but good virtues to discuss. Leaders with integrity are more concerned about their character than their reputation. Your reputation is merely who others think you are, but your character is who you really are.

Always wear your cloak of integrity and never leave home without your moral compass. An author wrote a short story about two small-time crooks trying to pull off a robbery. In the plan, one of the crooks was to dress up in a policeman's uniform and stand in front of the place to be robbed. That way, with him there, no one would be suspicious while his partner pulled off the heist itself. The story ended; however, with the partner dressed as a policeman apprehending and arresting the other one. Dressed as a cop, he started to act like one!

The further up, the corporate ladder you go, the deeper your roots must be planted. Always be firmly grounded when it comes to integrity. The branches of growing trees, not only reach higher, but their roots grow deeper. Strong, deep roots will anchor you firmly when the storms of ethical dilemma intensely blow your way. I challenge leaders to live and lead with integrity. It will not only benefit the people you lead, but also, you will enjoy more peace in your personal and professional life.

SECTION TWO

NAVIGATING LEADERSHIP AND UNCERTAIN TIMES

CHAPTER FIVE

THE FOUR SEASONS OF LEADERSHIP

Human history is a series of repeated cycles. Leadership, like the rest of our affairs, is cyclical in character. Understanding the different seasons of leadership can help you to remain focused and make the necessary transitions to get the results you want throughout the year.

THE LEADERSHIP CYCLE

The Leadership Cycle correlates with the "The Four seasons of Leadership."

1 Sometimes one season may last longer than another.

2 Sometimes in anyone season, there may be days reflective of another season.

SPRING – LEADERSHIP AWARENESS

Leadership Spring is the season of new beginnings and new growth. It is a time for sowing seeds. It's filled with great expectations; a promise of wonder. It spells **Leadership Awareness:** transitioning in a new role or assignment. Spring also comes with fresh ideas and projects, and we are ready to take on new challenges. In this leadership season, we are excited and optimistic, and our plans look achievable. During our leadership spring, we are strong and confident; resilient and moving forward. It's the no-fault stage where we "dream of happily-ever-after"; about saving the day. It is usually met with the least resistance from followers. You seem to have all the solutions and hold the missing key. It's very important at this stage to pull out the weeds—remove obstacles and have the right people on your team.

"From a small seed, a mighty trunk may grow" —Aeschylus

SUMMER – LEADERSHIP DEVELOPMENT

This season has the most activities and is marked with startling revelation as the heat soars. The leader is counted on to deliver results; growth in the bottom-line. There is a lot of pressure to meet objections. Your resiliency will be tested. The days are indeed longest and the nights are shortest. The realization on how heavy the responsibly is starts to sink in. Cracks in plans begin to surface, and conflict rises. It may mean revisiting plans and breaking down goals into smaller, realistic outcomes.

This is the season to nurture your investment. Your efforts during the summer are a leading indicator of what you will reap in the fall. More emphasis needs to be placed on team building. Do not expect to reap a high-performing team and a solid culture if you have not sown diligently. This is the time to invest in others and work hard on cultivating your team. It requires watering (coaching), sunlight (vision), care (mentoring), and feeding (communication) to build a strong root structure and foundation for continuous growth.

"Summertime is always the best of what might be" —Charles Bowden

AUTUMN – LEADERSHIP MATURITY

Leadership Autumn involves cooling / settling down. Energy from the summer begins to fade. Autumn brings the harvest and spells reality check. It's about performance. The hard work and drive from the summer leads to a harvest—it might be

below average, average, or above expectations– and, in many ways, the results will reflect the strategies employed in the summer. You will be held accountable for the results and will have to give account for your actions.

In Autumn, we collect a harvest and begin to ask ourselves if the harvest was what we expected or even what we needed.

Preparation for winter begins. It will mean analyzing results. Ask the following questions:

- ⮑ What can we **start doing** to improve our service, product, and company?

- ⮑ What should we **keep doing** that worked for us?

- ⮑ What can we **stop doing that** did not add value?

"Autumn carries more gold in its pocket than all the other seasons" —Jim Bishop

WINTER – LEADERSHIP REINVENTION AND DECLINE

Your winter can be short or long depending on how hard you worked during the spring. Winter is a time for reflection—to pause, refresh, rebuild, and renew. Look out for the occasional blizzards. It's a time of dormancy and replenishment; however, it involves planning for the next year by analyzing the Autumn "crop." Did you and your team perform as you planned? Recognition is key at this stage. Invest in filling any gaps; work on yourself and on your team. In winter, we must also plan and prepare for the next season of growth.

"Some people plant in the spring and leave in the summer. If you're signed up for a season, see it through. You don't have to stay forever, but at least, stay until you see it through" — Jim Rohn

The Law of the Harvest. Even though your efforts do not always yield visible results, keep sowing seeds. Your investment will pay off in the right season and at the right time. Times are changing, but one fact about life and leadership that is inevitable, is you reap what you sow.

CHAPTER SIX

LEADING CHANGE

Change is never easy. If you've ever tried to implement a change in your organization, you've learned it the hard way. When you try to change processes or incorporate new technologies, people often resist the change. The desire to maintain the familiar is in our nature, and it expresses itself in both direct and indirect resistance. Change is the one of the biggest challenges for any leader. Change creates disruption, conflict and fear. Change requires effort and adjustment. Without change, every organization is doomed to eventual failure. Change leadership has its own demands and requires a different set of competences in order to lead your people to a new place. Everyday leadership is not "a walk in the park." Putting it in perspective, you might think of it as the difference between peacetime and wartime leadership. Change leadership is not a one-off activity. Change requires continuous alignment and adaptation. **Change occurs as a process, not as an event.** Organizational change does not happen instantaneously because there was an announcement or a kick-off meeting. Individuals do not change just because they received an email or attended a training program. When we experience change, we move from what we have being doing through a period of transition to arrive at a desired new way of doing things.

Top executives surveyed by Development Dimensions International (DDI, 2007) identified the ability to motivate staff (35%), work well across cultures (34%), and facilitate change (32%) as critical leadership characteristics. Within the same report, only 11% of executives selected technical expertise as a leadership quality of the future.

The mistake that most organizations make is that they gave the systems and processes their primary attention whilst people were just secondary. **Change should be people-centred.** It should be about teamwork. Everyone needs to be onboard and moving in the same direction if this change effort is to be successful. Recent leadership research (Carter *et al.*, 2015) points out the significance of our interpersonal relationships in fostering effective team and organizational performance. Leadership is not a solo activity directed from the top. The most effective change leaders are connected with their people.

Resistance to change is the largest obstacle that leaders are faced with when initiating a change effort. A study by *Harvard Business Review* found that 66 percent of change initiatives fail to achieve their desired business outcomes.

THE FIVE MOST COMMON OBSTACLES TO CHANGE:

- ➲ Employee resistance

- ➲ Communication breakdown

- ➲ Insufficient time devoted to training

- ➲ Staff turnover during transition

- ➲ Cost exceeded budget

You need to inspire and guide your troops to see beyond their current roles, and look forward and work toward the future state. Change leadership is being able to manage your day-to-day activities while transitioning toward the changed business. Visible active leadership is the key ingredient of successful change. Change leadership entails thoughtful planning and sensitive implementation and, above all, involvement of the people affected by the changes. If you force change on people, normally, problems arise. Change must be realistic, achievable, and measurable.

10 IMPORTANT ASPECTS OF CHANGE LEADERSHIP INCLUDE:

1 **Create a shared vision**: A vision is your poster image of what you are working toward. The clearer, the better, such as:

⮑ We're going to improve our margins (okay, but vague)

⮑ We're going to double revenues within two years (more specific)

Sharing a vision is a central role of a leader. Leaders play a critical role when it comes to change. They must show personal commitment, and communicate a convincing vision. Inspiring and empowering people to accept change and belief in a shared vision is essential. You must provide a clear picture of the future and of what the change will bring. A vision gives people a bigger picture of what the future will be like. It helps them raise their hopes; it inspires them. When people are inspired, they are more prone to commit to a goal. *As a leader, you want people to make the vision their own.* This is an important step in bringing people together to work towards a common goal. Team members need to have a shared vision and a sense of ownership in order to be committed to the team.

Buddy Blanton, a principal program manager at Rockwell Collins, asked his team for some feedback on his leadership. He got some strong honest advice from his team about how he could be more effective in inspiring a shared vision. One of his direct reports said to him, "You would benefit by helping us, as a team, to understand how you got to your vision. We want to walk with you while you create the goals and vision, so we all get to the end vision together."

2 **Start at the top and involve every layer.** Because change is innately unsettling for people at all levels of an organization, when it is on the horizon, all eyes will turn to the leadership team for support and direction. The leaders themselves must embrace the new approaches first, both to challenge and to motivate the rest of the institution. They must speak with one voice and exemplify the desired behaviours. The public face must be one of unity. Acting independently can create confusion and a lack of commitment and interest in the change process. I have witnessed so many times the executive team saying one thing whilst the managers and supervisors say something else. Their actions and lack of interest indicate that they don't support or believe in the vision. You must be persistent about the change and support others at every opportunity until the change is complete. To succeed with the change in your company, you often ought to change the mindsets of people needed to accompany you on the road to promote and "sell" the change. These are the people who will help you in convincing other individuals with dialogue about the change, and eventually, in implementing the change. This requires investing

time to develop variety of relationships across the organization. It is all too easy to run individual fiefdoms and not operate as a team. It is not only enough to win over the executive team, but also, employees in the face of change.

We must also communicate a clear course that employees connect with and want to follow. This transparency must flow from the top. Ensuring alignment at this every level of the organisation is a critical step. Once the goals are agreed among leaders, they must cascade a shared vision clearly stating the specific role each individual plays in making the change happen. Leaders often fail to take into account the extent to which frontline people can make or break a change initiative. Early engagement at manylevels of the hierarchy will ensure that the process will be more efficient. When people are more invested when they've have been included in developing a plan. Ownership is best created by involving people in identifying problems and brainstorming solutions. This includes sharing ideas and best practices across the entire team. It is reinforced by rewards. These can be tangible (financial compensation) or psychological (recognition). Frontline people tend to be rich sources of knowledge about what problems need to be addressed and how to handle customers'reactions.

Meg Whitman, CEO of Hewlett-Packardand her senior team followed this principle in their transformation efforts. They sought to initiate a strong personal connection between the executive team and its employees by setting the example starting from the top. This included such actions as tearing down the barriers that surrounded the executive parking lot and moving top executives into cubicles. Through these efforts the company reinforced the original "HP Way" ethic in which the intrinsic quality of the work is as important as one's position in the hierarchy.

3 **Gap Analysis:** This is an important tool for determining what you need to do to meet the change objectives. *Assess the cultural landscape.* Identify the core values, beliefs and behaviours that must be taken into account for successful change to occur. Persuading people to change their behaviour won't suffice for transformation unless formal elements—such as structure and ways of operating are redesigned to support them. Determine what steps need to be taken in order to move from the current state to the desired future state. If your organization does not have the **structure** in place to support the people you will be driving, the change process will be a bumpy, lengthy process. The change must be integrated into your overall project plans, and not put together separately or in parallel. The challenge is to make change a part of the business plan and not an add-on that is managed independently.

It's also vital at this stage to conduct an **Impact Analysis**. It's absolutely crucial to brainstorm the major areas affected by the decision change, and then formulate:

➲ The actions you'll need to take to manage or mitigate these consequences

➲ The contingency strategy needed to manage the situation, should the negative consequences arise

⇒ People react in unexpected ways; there may be system problems and external environment shifts

Remember that few changes happen in isolation.

IBM recognized the need for such an approach in 2003 when rolling out a new initiative on culture. The leadership team had met intensively to access the current culture and determine the cultural traits that the organization would require moving forward. They then set up a website that was ran for a seventy two hour period, and where anyone in the company could post comments, concerns, suggestions, and responses. Leaders then made calculated changes based on the feedback they received and communicated clearly how the information they'd received was being integrated.

4 **Communicating the change**. It's important to give your team a chance to understand the importance of change. Help them to connect the big picture. Why is the change necessary? What will the future look like? And, how will you get there? It's important to clarify the rationale behind the change and connect the big picture to the purpose. **Explain how you see the impacton the people and not just the business**. Let them be a part of that process, so that they also feel a sense of ownership over the change. By working through the steps with your team, you're building joint ownership and commitment. Be sure that the team clearly understands your goals and objectives. Reinforce and clarify. Persistent communication, in many forms, is important to the success of any change effort. How you communicate the change vision can either ease or escalate fear.

Communication should be simple and heartfelt; thereby, speaking to anxieties, confusion and distrust. Supply realistic details of both the positives and negatives of the change, and provide key information on a consistent basis. Maintain regular review meetings and adapt the organization's meeting structure and agendas to support the improved processes. *As a leader, force yourself to be on the front lines*; this will definitely boost morale. Silence will be interpreted unfavourably, and gaps will be filled by the grapevine. Staff surveys are a helpful to understand how people view the change, provided you allow people to complete them anonymously. By acting upon the findings you may ease mistrust among staff. **Be open to discussion**, and think about ways employee's ideas can be integrated. Allow dialogue, as it will help alleviate the anxiety that change brings about in people. They must be guided through the process. Powerful and sustained change requires constant communication, not only through the rollout, but after the major elements of the plan are in place.

5   **Address the "human side."** Make the logical and emotional case together. Human beings respond to calls to action that engage their hearts, as well as their minds. It makes them feel as if they are a part of something substantial. *Most employees resist change due to job insecurity, mistrust of management, increased workload, and fewer opportunities for advancement.* Leaders must show commitment to the change

initiative, but above all, to the people who are affected by the change. This requires relationship building; thus, leaders must display authenticity, integrity, empathy, and humility in their approach. Change and influence are intricately linked. Influence is about gaining not only compliance, but also, the commitment necessary to successfully drive change.

It's important to assess and address how the changes will affect people. Let employees know that you understand the range of emotions associated with change. Personal losses to them should be openly acknowledged. Show care and concern and allow them time to grieve. Treat the past with respect. *Allow people to take a piece of the past with them,* as this will allow a smoother acceptance to change. Your ability to navigate change is built on trust in the decisions they make. If your employees trust your judgment, the process of change will be easier. The more people trust you, the quicker you can understand their motivations and drivers and deal with issues that may arise. Trust is about getting people to work with you and believe in the vision and change efforts.

6 **Understand how your team will respond.** Building a strong understanding of human behaviour is one the greatest challenges associated with leadership. This requires us as leaders to build a mindfulness of others' motivational drivers, which is often related to their personality. Having an understanding of your team's attitude toward change will provide you with additional insight on how to best guide the transition. Be aware of people's strengths and weaknesses. Not everyone will

welcome change. Take the time to comprehend the people you are dealing with, and how and why they feel like they do, before you act. Help team members focus on what's important and get rid of distractions. Age is another factor. Erik Erikson's fascinating Psychosocial Theory is helpful for understanding that people's priorities and motivations are different depending on their stage of life. The more you understand people's needs, the better you will be able to manage change.

"Acceptance makes an incredible fertile soil for the seeds of change." —Steve Maraboli

THE THREE INDIVIDUAL ATTITUDES TOWARD CHANGE

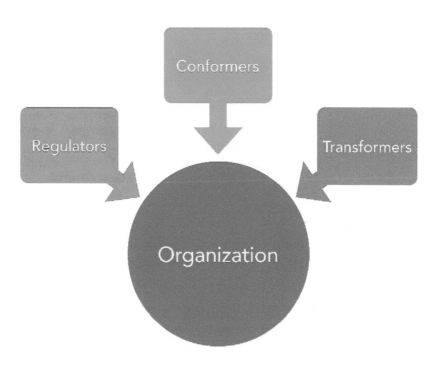

➲ **Regulators:** They *fail to see any positive outcomes* and keep challenging the process of change. They value habits and complacency. They do not want to step out of their comfort zone, so they look for every opportunity to blame and criticize. They secretly harbour fear of the unknown. They have a hard time in coming to terms with the change, as they always revert to and compare the present with the past.These individuals would require more training and focus groups to discuss their concerns.

➲ **Conformers**: They are *interested, but not totally convinced*; therefore, would need persuasion. They want to see what's in it for them. They rely on information, and can swing on either side. Hence, more emphasis needs to be placed on these marginal constituents to get them actively involved in the change process. Eventually, when the change is implemented, they go along with it *"just because it's policy."*

➲ **Transformers:**These are otherwise known as the experimenters—the free spirited. They openly welcome and champion the change, always eagerly providing suggestions and feedback. They quickly embrace the principle of "out with the old - in with the new" and easily adapt to the new environment.

The goal is to develop a powerful change agents network. It's important to get the right people in place who are fully committed to the change initiative and who have the power influence to drive the change effort at all levels. Informal leaders must be identified before they can be engaged. By mapping out connections, you can complement the formal org chart with one that enables you to lead outside the lines. Is there someone on your team resistant to change? Looking at them through the lens of empathy can help to see their point of view. Change leadership that drives high performance requires "leading from behind." A change leader's role is to guide and lead their team on a better journey. You need to understand and see how your team is moving ahead in the journey; only then can you help guide the team by re-enforcing their direction and changing the course when needed. It's important to match passionate employees with important projects in order to drive change on a basic level.

7. **Training and Coaching:** Use hands-on training sessions to achieve understanding, involvement and commitment. Change, such as new structures, policies and acquisitions, creates new systems and environments. Assess training needs driven by the change. By comparing existing skills and competencies with the skills you want people to have, you can make an informed decision about the type of training each person or team needs and provide the necessary training. Additionally, remove obstacles to empower people. Make sure team members have everything they need to do their work. Train, coach, and mentor personnel where necessary, and invite continued involvement in the processes. Listen to the concerns of those close to the front lines, as their insights and experience are critical to execution and success. Training should be properly structured and not rushed. This should build confidence around the change effort.

Encourage your employees to think of new ways of doing things. Meaning and Purpose are fundamental to keeping your team engaged. The Australian Institute of Management, undertook a comprehensive national study in September and October 2006, to determine the main factors that influence employees'engagement. Almost 3,000 people participated in the survey: 61.9% said, 'A sense of meaning and purpose in my job keeps me engaged', while 30.1% said, 'Reward and recognition keep me engaged.

8. **Give careful attention to the Implementation Stage**: For organizational change that entails new actions, objectives, and processes for a group or a team of people, you need to ensure that there is a common framework, language (common set of definitions), tools, approaches, and that everyone is familiar with. Many companies fall short in this area. Change leadership requires a healthy dose of listening and conflict management; truly listening where practical, and utilizing the information to shape the solution. To effectively lead change, we need to be intuitive. William Duggan (2007) terms this 'strategic intuition'—reconnecting existing nuggets of insight in new ways in order to produce innovative ideas. There may be a period of some confusion, as the move from the old to the new way of doing things occurs. It will involve a transition period. Remember that change is not a sprint to the finish line. In order to gain efficiency, people will have to take on new tasks and responsibilities, which entails a learning curve. This process can be lengthy and most certainly will not happen in a couple of days. It will take time for people to feel comfortable and to fully adopt

change initiative. The question is who is accountable for effective change management in your organization: Managers or experts (internally or externally)? Unless your managers are accountable for making sure that change happens comprehensively, they won't develop their skills. In organizations, the manager's role is to interpret, communicate, and empower, not to order and control, which nobody responds to well. They must manage the change in a way that employees can cope with it. The leader has a responsibility to facilitate and empower change, not merely convey and implement policy from above, which does not work.

9 **Rewards and Recognition**. If leaders are to promote and sustain positive behavioural change, a simultaneous change in the performance management process must be accompanied. Leaders should be clear about

the underlying behaviours that will best support the new way of doing things, and find opportunities to perfect those behaviours. Rewards and incentives are reinforcers of behaviours. Without positive reinforcement in the midst of change, engagement and employee morale are at risk. Create short-term wins and celebrate successes. For organizational success, it's critical for employees to execute on strategic objectives promptly. You want to retain top talent and you also want your employees to stay engaged during the transition period, so that productivity does not take a plunge. It's important to tailor rewards or motivational tools to ensure that they resonate with the target audience. Younger generations like the Millennials can have vastly different reward systems than Gen-Xers or Baby Boomers. Recognition is also one of the most important rewards that employees can receive. Focus on creating a culture of recognition. Leaders should always be on the lookout to spot good behaviours, and be quick to openly praise the recipient of these.

10 **Monitoring and Evaluation: Prepare for the unexpected.** The stage is crystallizing the adaptation of a new standard as norm. Change will only reach its full effect if it's made permanent, so every effort must be made to cement it. No change program goes completely according to plan. It's essential to recognize that the change journey is not a straight line. Leaders need to make the adjustments necessary to maintain momentum and drive. The organization may relapse to its former ways of doing things at this point unless the changes are reinforced. Regularly review progress at

the team and individual levels. This is where you verify the degree of adoption of the changed environment. Leaders are so eager to claim success that they don't take the time to find out what isn't working and to adjust their next steps accordingly. Are employees moving forward with the change or are they holding on to the old ways? How are we monitoring and measuring their progress? Feedback is important at this stage. It's also essential that the performance management system should also be reviewed to confirm if it is effective. Constantly share performance expectations and progress with team members. Showing employees the big picture and where they fit into it will drive momentum. The change process must be intertwined with the performance management system to ensure sustainability.

"If we don't change, we don't grow. If we don't grow, we aren't really living." —Anatole France

An international consumer products corporation had made a commitment to reducing costs. Leaders designed a thorough change template and implemented it comprehensively. The company wanted to make sure that the team understood the ongoing requirement of this commitment even though results revealed that the goals were being achieved. So, they rolled out a system of pulse surveys and organized focus groups to describe the case for change and the new behaviours desired. The first phase of surveys found that only sixty percent of employees understood the message. The company then called on informal leaders to play a greater role in clarifying the initiative. They continued to run these surveys and focus groups to measure the result until a greater majority of the staff had shown they were prepared, and the change was adapted into the organization.

We are living in a time of continual disruption in business. This comes with rapid change in all areas of business and the economy. Successful businesses are constantly changing. They're introducing new offerings based on customer demand, expanding into new markets, and making product updates to improve their bottom line. To survive in today's world, organizations must be willing to embrace change to be proactive change (before being incited by an event and not just reactive (in response to an event). The winners and losers of this global competition are determined by one factor: change.

CHAPTER SEVEN

LEADING IN A RECESSION

Recession requires sacrifice and extraordinary effort by everyone. Leaders must work with employees to provide a realistic vision of the way forward for the organization.

STRATEGIES EMPLOYED BY COMPANIES:

- ⮊ Shutting down underperforming business units

- ⮊ Paying suppliers more slowly

- ⮊ Slowing capital projects

- ⮊ Not paying bonuses

- ⮊ Job downgrades

- ⮊ Hiring freeze and using temporary workers

- ⮊ Lay offs

Leaders often focus on operational efficiency and adopt short-term survival strategies. Sadly, many employees complain that management is overworking them, demanding extended hours, intimidating them with more layoffs, and not communicating information. Especially prevalent is the preaching that those who are still employed with the company should be especially motivated and work harder simply because they still have a job. Staff can become more disenchanted and make the decision to be highly committed or highly uncommitted. Unfortunately, such practices can lead to fear, demotivation, mistrust of management, and reduced quality of work, all of which will affect the bottom line.

In this period, communication is key. People hate uncertainty. Interpret and communicate at different levels in different ways to help people make sense of where you are headed and why. It is essential that you keep two-way communications timely and reliable; otherwise, rumours will be spreading like wildfire through the grapevine. Leaders must step up their visibility in the organization. During tough times, the top leaders need to be highly visible to provide a sense of reassurance and stability to employees. They inspire the team by communicating their belief in the success of the company. Leaders must also show that they are listening and that they welcome employee feedback.

Management must resist the urge to overcompensate by micromanaging and adopting scientific management to increase productivity and conformity. Avoid interrupting the workflow with excessive staff meetings and demands for additional progress reports. Effective leaders inspire loyalty and good will in others because they themselves act with integrity. They are confident in uncertainty and grounded in fundamental principles and values rather than relying on quick fixes. They provide a sense of direction for the organization and encourage a collaborative response to adversity. They let their team know that they are available to offer support when required, and they are not afraid to apologize or show vulnerability.

In an article in Chief Executive Magazine, John Kador wrote: "Apology is not a get-out-of-jail-free card, but it's less costly than the alternatives. Leaders who apologize just have better outcomes than those who don't."

It's absolutely central that companies develop strategies to manage their people through the crisis if they are to survive and prosper in the long term.

It's critical in this period to:

- **Re-publicize your Employee Assistance Programme** (EAP) counselling services. A recession can be very stressful, and the effects felt in both our personal and professional lives.

- **Conduct Employee surveys.** Do surveys of a sample of your key workers employees in order to identify their issues and concerns. Then, you will be able to confirm if employee morale is rising or declining.

- **Keep your team engaged** and committed to the organization. Continue to employ team building activities.

- **Rewards and Recognition**. Find low-cost ways of rewarding positive behaviour, such as sponsoring breakfast treats, pizza lunches, or gift cards. Frequently thank employees both publicly and privately.

In certain situations where things are unfavourable and a downsizing strategy may be utilized, as the leader, you have the power to make the whole process more humane and not just callous. Those employees who are left will always be suspicious of management. *Certain changes may be non-negotiable, but how you lead it makes all the difference*. Leaders must show compassion. Employee commitment, motivation, and trust in the organization will suffer if leaders and managers are inconsiderate about the way they treat people in a recession.

Everyone is looking on and you will be judged by how you treat those who have to leave the organization. During large-scale layoffs, morale and productivity can plummet. The most common form of stress that employees face is what is known as "survivor's guilt." It results from the fact that "you" have a job and some of your colleagues don't. Managers must be made aware of the phenomenon, show empathy with the survivor and offer support where needed.

Most successful leaders balance the obvious need for cost-cutting with the investment required to take calculated risks out in the market. They monitor the actions of competitors and industry leaders to learn from them. A lack of focus on opportunity including those that might be seen as slightly risky will eventually lead to failure. The only likely result of excessive retrenchment is the ultimate demise of the business.

In the 2000 economic downturn, Sony cut its workforce by 11%, its research & development expenditures by 12%, and its capital expenditures by 23%. The cuts helped Sony increase its profit margin from 8% in 1999 to 12% in 2002, but growth in its sales tumbled from an average of 11% in the three years before the recession to 1% thereafter. In fact, Sony has struggled since then to regain momentum.

There may be a need to improve a company's image. Bad public relations as a result of negative press coverage from large layoffs can impact your future recruiting, brand image, and subsequent sales. Some of the most successful companies in the midst of an economic downturn invest in **Corporate Social Responsibility**; it's about giving to the community even if it's in a small way. Pick a current issue, declare a clear goal, and mobilize your resources. Make sure it is something you easily sustain. Show that you genuinely care. Get employees involved. One of the greatest benefits of promoting social responsibility is the positive environment it encourages for employees.

A midsized steel plant company was laying off workers. It got very ugly. The union and employees were protesting and even the government got involved.The company was eventually fined by the *Industrial Court* for the procedure it used in laying off over 500 workers. To offset this negative public image, the company's executive management team started to take an active interest in the community. Many times representatives were seen on television, giving out beds and food supplies to victims of house fires, and any mishaps that happened in the community, they were present and supporting even though in a small way.

A LONG-TERM STRATEGY

When a company is struggling, it's logical that leaders take the short-term view, focusing on quick gains to cut costs and increase short-term revenue. However, leaders should focus efforts on investing in research and development programs and other projects needed to prepare for a recovery. Be creative in your problem-solving methods, seek new knowledge, look beyond the traditional metrics of today, and identify what is over-valued and under-valued at your organization. In this period, the more emphasis should be placed on customers. Get closer to customers who may be ignored by competitors. Companies that master the balance between cutting costs to survive today and investing to grow tomorrow perform better after a recession.

Office Depot and Staples took contrary approaches to cost management during the 2000 recession. Office Depot cut 6% of its workforce, but it couldn't lessen operating costs considerably. Its sales growth fell from 19% before the recession to 8% after—five percentage points below Staples' post-recession sales growth rate. By contrast, Staples closed down some underperforming facilities, but increased its workforce by 10% during the recession. Simultaneously, the company contained its operating costs and came out of the recession stronger and more profitable than before the recession. Its sales doubled from $7.1 billion in 1997 to $14.6 billion in 2003 while Office Depot's rose by about 50% from $8.7 billion to $13.4 billion. On average, Staples was about

30% more profitable than its archival in the three years after that recession.

"Never waste a good crisis." —*Benjamin Netanyahu, Prime Minister of Israel*

It is important that leaders see the recession as an opportunity to refine long-term strategy, forge new alliances, and look for customer niches, which they can better serve. Turn negatives into positives. A recession provides the leader with the platform to make changes that would otherwise have been resisted. Many people look at a recession as something to get through until they can go back to business as usual. But, business as usual will never be the same. Be aggressive in the marketplace. It's time to create the changes that move the market in your favour instead of waiting and responding to the changes as they take place.

Great businesses focus on short-term survival, but have a steadfast eye on the medium to long-term and a strong focus on post-recessionary times. The key to this is keeping the right people and thinking about engagement to ensure they stay after the recession lifts.

CHAPTER EIGHT

LEADING IN TIMES OF A CRISIS

Every organization is vulnerable to crises, and leaders are suddenly confronted with major challenges. A poor response to those events could, in severe cases, result in the loss of the business. The responsibility of the leader is to put any crisis in appropriate stand point and to lead people out of it. A crisis demands real leadership. Only through real leadership (inspiring a shared vision, making tough choices and facing setbacks) does a company or a society survive. According to Stanford University researchers, the single most important leadership trait among the top Fortune 1000 CEO's was their ability to deal with a crisis. The measure of a leader is often tested during a crisis. Your leadership legacy may ultimately be judged by how well you navigated people through a crisis.

Every company should have a crisis plan that considers the following:

- *What could go wrong?* You can't think of everything, but this is imperative to help the company understand what types of issues could turn into a true crisis and to properly prepare.

- *Who's in charge?* There needs to be a designated chain of command. When a crisis hits, you shouldn't be wasting time trying to figure out who has what role or responsibilities.

- *What's our strategy? You should develop a contingency plan; a* course of action designed to respond effectively; *however, it should not be iron clad. Leave room for flexibility.* Although negative events probably come to mind first, a good contingency plan should also address positive events that might disrupt operations, such as a very large order.

"The ultimate measure of a man is not where he stands in moments of comfort and convenience, but where he stands in times of challenge and controversy." —*Martin Luther* King, Jr.

THE JOHNSON & JOHNSON EXAMPLE

In 1982, Johnson & Johnson faced a major crisis when its pain reliever, Tylenol, was tampered with in a few locations. The media coverage sparked rumours of tampering on an enormous scale, presenting the company with a major emergency on its hands. A total of seven people died in the Chicago area after taking cyanide-laced Tylenol capsules. Johnson & Johnson's leadership believed that the best way to confront the crisis was with an authentic communication platform. The firm promised that Tylenol would be safe on the shelves of the nation's stores or it would not be there. This led to them removing the product from shelves nationally, so that there could be no risk of any more poisoning. Consequently, the tampering was isolated and ended. Before the 1982 crisis, Tylenol controlled more than thirty-five percent of the over-the-counter pain reliever market; only a few weeks after the deaths, that number plunged to less than eight percent. The dismal situation, both in terms of human life and business, made it urgent that the leadership respond promptly and convincingly. Within a year, and after an investment of more than $100 million, Tylenol had regained more than 80 percent of its market share and became, once again, the nation's favourite over-the-counter pain reliever. Critics who had early proclaimed the demise of the brand, Tylenol, were now praising the company's treatment of the matter.

JOHNSON AND JOHNSON LEADERSHIP RESPONSE TO CRISIS:

- ➾ They sincerely apologized and assumed responsibility by ensuring public safety.

- ➾ They expressed concern for the impact that the situation had on customers and the general public.

- ➾ They put the customer first. They showed the concern was genuine. Their actions matched their words. Johnson & Johnson CEO, James Burke, swiftly ordered a recall of 31 million bottles, which cost the company a staggering $50 million.

- ➾ They communicated openly. They opened the doors to the media to give the public an assurance of full transparency.

- ➾ They made a commitment to identify the underlying factors that caused the situation to happen and addressed them.

- ➾ They voiced confidence that this situation did not reflect poorly on the company overall.

- ➾ They prevented the crisis from recurring. A crisis, by definition, is a one-time-only, unexpected, negative event. They took the necessary steps (introduced tamperproof packaging) to ensure the crisis does not repeat itself.

CRISIS···NEW CRISIS···NEW CRIS

"In a moment of crisis, reactions set the leaders apart from the followers." –Peter Stark

HOW LEADERS RESPOND IN MOMENTS OF CRISIS:

1. **Take control of the situation.** Be visible, present, and attentive. Leaders must think and act positively in a crisis. **Lead with confidence.** Your presence brings much needed reassurance that things will be fine. Be visible during and after the crisis to your colleagues, customers, stockholders, and communities. If it's possible, go to the scene of the disaster or visit those that have been affected. At the same time, leaders must know when it is time to give up control. Different situations call for different approaches. The well documented failure of the then Governor of Louisiana to allow the federal

government quick access and control over the response efforts after Hurricane Katrina led to much higher levels of destruction and damage than was necessary.

2 **Keep people informed**. The foundation of any crisis response is communication. The first task is to prevent widespread panic. You must take control of the situation. Take a moment to figure out what's going on. When a crisis hits, the first thing you do is get the facts. Then, you have to resolve what you can communicate publicly based on legal and other restraints. Finally, *respond in a timely fashion*. The longer you wait, people will get the information they are looking for from other sources. Communication must be regular, truthful, and frequent. Leaders must continually focus on crafting and sending clear, unambiguous communications with minimal error for misinterpretation. In the absence of authoritative and accurate information, rumours flourish and people driven by emotions exaggerate happenings.

3 **Stay calm and collected.** Leaders have to control their emotions under pressure. Many people lose their cool when a crisis happens. One of the finest examples of leadership during a crisis was former New York City Mayor, Rudolph Giuliani's management of 9/11. Giuliani, showed what a leader is supposed to do in a crisis. Asked how he managed to stay calm amid the chaos, Giuliani related that staying calm would allow him to think and make better decisions. Acting in a panic would lead to bad decisions. He stated, "Leaders have to control their emotions under pressure. Much of your ability to get people to do what they have to do is going to depend on what they perceive when they look

at you and listen to you. They need to see someone who is stronger than they are, but human too."

4 **Show both Sympathy and Empathy** without getting too emotional. It's important to show your human side. All eyes are on you, but if you break down, everyone else will. We tend to confuse empathy with sympathy. Sympathy is a feeling of pity or sorrow for the distress of another whilst empathy is really being able to understand the needs of others. It means that you are aware of their feelings and how it impacts them. Empathy is an important component of effective relationships and is indeed a valued currency. Empathy allows leaders to develop and maintain relationships with those they lead. Be aware of how this incident is not just affecting those externally, but those internally in the organization as well. After the initial first few days of the 9\11 horror, Giuliani was able to show both empathy and optimism. He was empathetic in the fact that he grieved along with all the other citizens for the tremendous loss of life. He sometimes attended multiple funerals during the weeks after the attacks.

5 **Inspire a Shared Vision**: Instil **Hope**—when a crisis happens and fear reigns, it's the leader's job to overthrow fear and bring hope. Giuliani, with his words during some of his press conferences about 9/11, gave Americans hope that they would meet this challenge and overcome it. He was also optimistic in telling New Yorkers that they, although it would take time, would bounce back. He let the people who lived in the city know how strong and resilient they were, and that they would get through this together (Forbes, 2011).

Most people just want to get through a crisis and forget about it. Leaders must educate themselves and their entire organizations to be better prepared for the next crisis they face. A **post-event analysis,** often called a **debrief session** should be held. A debrief is a well-structured and comprehensive analysis that reviews the actions taken, decisions made, successes and failures, and lessons learned to apply in the future. With a systematic debriefing process, leaders educate themselves and their entire team to be better prepared for the next crisis they face.

It's difficult to predict exactly when a crisis will occur and, although we all hope a crisis never befalls us, in today's environment, you're likely to deal with far more than just one crisis in your career. Sooner or later, unforeseen, unpleasant challenges will arise. However, leaders must be prepared to face the unexpected. Remember, as a leader, you are like a lighthouse to the ships lost at sea. People are depending on you in difficult times to steer and anchor the ship in a safe harbour.

CHAPTER NINE

LEADING WITH STRATEGIC THINKING

Most companies have leaders with the strong operational skills, but they lack people in positions of power with the know-how, experience, and confidence required to tackle innovative problems and lead change. Many leaders and organizations are tactical and operational, few are strategic. Effective and productive strategic leadership requires different perspective and skills than those required by day to day operational leadership.

Strategic skills are not needed only in time of organizational growth but during the time of crisis when resources are scarce. Strategy is about predicting and planning for the future. We used to think that strategy was predicting what might happen in the marketplace over the next couple of years, and planning for this probable future by developing goals, actions and allocating resources. However, in the 21st century, we're faced with uncertainty and ambiguity and major disruptions. So, it's not enough to predict the future; we need to invent it. (van der Laan 2008, Raimond 1996)

A 2015 PricewaterhouseCoopers (PwC) study of 6,000 senior executives, conducted using a research methodology developed by David Rooke, of Harthill Consulting, and William Torbert, of Boston University, revealed just how prevalent this shortfall is. Respondents were asked a series of open-ended questions; their answers revealed their leadership inclinations, which were then analyzed to determine which types of leaders were most evident. Only eight percent of the respondents turned out to be strategic leaders or those effective at leading transformations.

A company's ability to create new products or new ways to differentiate itself from the competition is a fundamental component to success. Yet, most companies typically continue to seek growth with ever-greater investments in advertising and promotion, or additions to personnel. On the other hand, today's winning companies embed innovation in their business culture, operations, and in their strategic plans.

Research also suggests that for many organisational leaders, given the pressures of shareholders, regulatory environments, financial markets, their product market, and internal /external stakeholders, it's more expedient to take conservative managerialist approach (van der Laan 2013). The company's top executives aren't acting strategically. The gap; thus, comes to light only when a company faces a major challenge to its traditional way of doing business, and they discover the current leadership isn't up to the task.

Strategy was originally branded in the year 1810 as the "Art of a General." Before a General engaged an enemy in battle, he would take a position on high ground overlooking the battle to observe the arrangement of the opposing side and to dictate his stratagem to his Lieutenants. Viewing the battlefield was a way to gather data, better known currently as 'intelligence gathering', which enhanced decision-making and outcomes. In today's world, in the realm of business, leaders are like the Generals on the battlefield who formulate and execute strategic objectives more conducive to the marketplace. A well designed and implemented strategy is essential for organizational long-term success.

A strategic plan acts as a road map and a long term approach to achieving the organization's goals and objectives. It essentially tells an organization who it is, where it is going, and how it's going to get there. It helps an organization decide whether to expand operations or diversify, or whether to form a joint venture.

Strategic planning is a process, not an event. It is defined as the process of diagnosing an organization's environment, deciding the vision and mission, developing overall goals, creating and selecting general strategies, and allocating resources to achieve the organization's goals. Its objective is to align an organization's activities with its environment resulting in its continuing survival and effectiveness.

In order to be successful, you need to be strategic. There is always room for improvement and growth of your business. No business today can survive if it hopes to continue doing what it did one yearago. The right strategy allows each business to reach its optimum potential. Strategic leaders not only manage daily operations and solve current problems, they also foresee and carve out that future. Being a strategic leader starts with being a strategic thinker. Strategic thinking is set on a deep understanding of the complex relationship between the organization and its environment. Strategic leaders treat failures as a strong foundation on which to improve and identify patterns, connections, and key issues. Strategic leadership requires leaders to think and act in a way that promotes an enduring success of an organization. The goal of the strategic leader is to drive the organization on a path in which it can thrive in the long run.

In today's world, **we need leaders who embody both visionary leadership and strategic leadership**. Visionary leaders— those who see the big picture, and strategic leaders—those who create the plan are essential for the development and growth of an organization. Visionary leaders tend to be your type of leaders who can cast the vision with great enthusiasm and confidence. Strategic leaders break down the vision into workable and measurable action steps, which produces the vision. The strategic leader is the one who puts the puzzle together. The vision needs a strategic plan. Strategic leaders thrive on creating the plan and seeing it come into existence. Strategy is not a vision statement or a mission statement. Strategy is a unique approach. Strategic leadership is the *ability to think, influence, and act in ways that uniquely positions an organization for ongoing success.*

HERE ARE THE 10 ESSENTIAL QUALITIES OF STRATEGIC LEADERS:

1 **Vision:** Strategic leaders focus on the future. They keep their eyes on big the picture. Strategic actions take place over long periods of time. A strategic leader operates with a far reaching agenda, integrating short term results and long term focus.

2 **Awareness:** Strategic awareness isn't just about forecasting and reading data, but about figuring out how to take action on that information in order to achieve better results and contribute to the organization's mission. Strategic leaders have peripheral vision; they wander outside of the current frame of their business and bust boundaries. Strategic thoughts and actions is a regular part of their daily routine.

3 **Risk:** They regularly seek out challenges for themselves and find ways to push their team out of their comfort zones. They understand at a deep level that current success won't last forever, and it can lead to complacency, so they challenge people to experiment and take risks. However, they make every effort to take risks with the right level of exposure.

4 **Innovation:** Such leaders identify new opportunities to transform the organization. They lead with an eye toward what's next. The strategic plan is a plan to **innovate**. There must be a constant pursuit of fresh market insights. Such leaders aggressively scan the environment for patterns and clues about events that could reveal opportunities or pose threats to their organization's success. They also scan for disruptive technologies or market players that have the power to reshape their industries. They are navigators and not just map-readers.

5 **The Ability to Interpret and Communicate:** Strategic leaders spend a lot of time receiving information, filtering it down to the essential matters, and sending it out to staff effectively to produce results. The communication skills of such a leader must be excellent. They break down information into bite size pieces for staff to easily digest and use such language whereby they could clearly understand the vision. As Albert Einstein stated "If you can't explain it simply, you don't understand it well enough."

6   **They are Driven**: A Strategic leader is a driver of organizational change. Not only do they have a vision for the future but also the passion needed to create momentum and excitement. They have the drive needed when change becomes elusive and difficult. These leaders are not afraid to take decisive action that is consistent with the direction of the company's strategy even in the face of complexity and ambiguity.

7   **Relationship Building:** Strategic leaders enroll others in the journey. Strategy is a team sport. It's not a one man show; it takes an army of team players moving in the same direction. They know if they don't inspire others, people will resist them. They are good at selling new ideas and voluntarily getting others to sign up. The best strategic leaders build positive relationships both inside and outside the organization. The goal is to harness connections in order to create new business relationships and opportunities for the company.

8   **Growth Mind-set:** They are voracious learners. Being a strategic leader means you have to be hungry for new ideas. They learn everything about the market, competition, product and keep abreast of technology. They are teachers and developers. They focus on building skill sets and the required behaviours that are

needed to propel future growth; and are committed to teaching and transforming the organization and people.

9 **Embrace Diversity**: Many organizations include diversity, but do not put it to work. Diversity without inclusiveness only helps to build self-interest groups. These leaders realize that diversity adds a positive dimension to problem solving and brilliant insights can come from others around. They consider new and even non-conventional ideas objectively and explore relevant possibilities.They welcome and embrace different perspectives.

10 **Accountability**: Strategic leaders hold themselves and others accountable for achieving goals.They see failure as part of the process but in the end they require performance. They are not overly demanding or critical, but they make expectations quite explicit. They celebrate progress each step of the way and inject excitement into the process.

As a leader, your **strategic thinking skills and acumen** are fundamental in shaping powerful strategies for organizational growth. Strategic Acumen is being 'aware' of oncoming stimuli and responding appropriately thereby capturing early momentum and an advantage. The U.S. president, General Dwight D. Eisenhower (1890 - 1969) was fond of saying, "It's about the planning, not the plan. This requires real time observation, quick intelligence gathering, and calculating your next move. Some people talk about *foresight competence* as a mix of envisioning, systems and complexity thinking, and risk awareness (van der Laan 2008), others see it as a process of collecting intelligence, interpreting it, and developing action plans (Horton 1999).

STRATEGIC PLANNING STEPS

Strategic planning has a basic overall framework. It is the process of addressing the following questions:

- Where are we?

- Where do we want to be?

- How do we get there?

1   **Analysis of the Current State**. Identify strategic issues to address. For an accurate picture of where your business currently is, conduct a SWOT analysis. Use facts, trends and data to support your assessment. Strengths—Weaknesses—Opportunities—Threats

(SWOT). SWOT analysis is one of the effective analytical tools to evaluate a situation. The situation may be strategic related or tactical related. SWOT Analysis forms one of the key critical success factors in a Strategic Planning Process. SWOT analysis provides an efficient way to analyze the range of factors that influence your operation, and can give valuable guidance in making decisions about what to do next. It also provides a highly effective way to get your key personnel involved in the decision-making process.

Example of organization's current state:

⮑ ABC Company has 5% of market share.

⮑ ABC Company has customer satisfaction scores of 65.

Vision is a very important aspect in ensuring that the work of strategy creation is never complete. A strong vision should be maintained, as well as specific success measures.

2 **Strategy formulation** is where the strategy is developed and the strategic plan is documented. Focus on where you want to take the organization over time. **The strategic plan** is the roadmap that helps leaders and their teams navigate the journey. The fundamental purpose of strategic planning is to align a company's mission and vision with its core values, and chart a path forward that will deliver desired results over a sustained period of time. Even if your organization already has a well-defined mission, vision, and core values statements, they should be reviewed

and used as guideposts throughout the strategic planning process. Objectives, goals, strategies, and measures define the roadmap to get your organization from where it is today to the desired vision you have articulated. Thorough analytics and insightful strategic thinking are important when developing a plan.

Example of organization's objection:

⮑ ABC Company will have a 25% market share by 2020.

⮑ ABC Company will have a customer satisfaction rate of 85 by 2020.

Strategic planning should not be an ivory tower exercise. It is a catalyst for collaboration and innovation needed to drive improved results. Remember, perfection is often the enemy of progress, and the strategic plan is a work in progress. The planning process is rarely simple and, due to organizational complexities, it can be easy to leave customers out of planning conversations. Are you in sync with customers? Customers are the most important *part* of your business. Take the time to bring relevant customer insights to the planning process. Customer expectations change quickly. The biggest mistake you can make is to ignore their rapidly evolving expectations. As Henry Ford said, "If I had asked people what they wanted, they would have said faster horses." Strategic planning should be a people-process more than a paper-process. Don't get caught up in complicated planning techniques. To have any chance at implementation, the plan must clearly articulate goals, action steps, responsibilities and precise deadlines. The critical actions move a strategic plan from a document on the shelf to actions that drive business growth. A strategic leader must build a sense of citizenship among the members of the team. Let them know what role they will play and encourage their input. The end goal is to generate a sense of comfort and acceptance among team members, resulting in a sense of ownership across the organization.

Hamel and Prahalad, (2005), talked about how important it is to dream big. Although strategic planning is billed as a way of becoming more future oriented, most managers when pressed will admit that their strategic plans reveal more about today's problems than tomorrow's opportunities.

What are your goals for the organization? Are you thinking about meeting the competition? Are you thinking about new markets and new opportunities? Managers tend to have a lake mentality whilst strategic leaders have an ocean mentality. Putting together a strategy places some real demands on a leader's ability to think in the widest sense. As a leader, it's necessary to develop the ocean mentality in your thinking process. You have to be able to view the strategy in its entirety and see how all parts of it interconnect. **"Avoid short-sighted vision." Big, Hairy, Audacious Goals (BHAG)** was made famous by Jim Collins and Porras (1996), "a true BHAG is clear and compelling, serves as a unifying focal point of effort, and acts as a clear catalyst for team spirit. It has a clear finish line, so the organization can know when it has achieved the goal; people like to shoot for finish lines."

These are great examples of BHAG's:

- ➲ Google: Organize the world's information and make it universally accessible and useful.

- ➲ Microsoft: A computer on every desk and in every home.

- ➲ Twitter: To become 'the pulse of the planet'.

3 **Assess your assets**. A strategic plan also helps business leaders determine where to spend time and money. The *strategic leader has a well-defined vision for the future*.They balance the present with the future in making resource and operational decisions. The third aspect for the strategic leader is assessing your assets. Strategy and culture are intimately intertwined. Don't just blindly follow best practices from your industry; other organizations' experiences may not be relevant to your own. Organizations are unique, complex, and diverse. Consider the specific needs of your organization, so it becomes your road map for success. Be realistic about what you can invest. Your assets will consist of your talent pool, and the available resources to get the job done. The key to a successful strategic plan is: Focus. Every company has limited resources, and strategy is all about effectively deploying those resources where they will have the most impact. Enlist the people. Everyone must understand the plan and his or her individual role in the change process. Alignment of employees and management is critical. If the senior team is not 100% committed to the strategic direction of the organization, the plan will fail. A strategic leader must consider their collective team's talent in **arranging**

assets. Clinical Psychologist, Dr. Henry Cloud notes, "It's about leading the 'right people', empowering them to find and do the 'right things' in the 'right way' at the 'right times.' In this phase, you must assess the strengths and weaknesses of your team, and rearrange your team members in a way to acquire optimum results. Strategic leaders see themselves as coaches and mentors. They bring clarity despite organizational and analytical complexity. They harness their power to connect people, resources, and ideas in new ways.

4 **Strategic Implementation and Execution:** Communicate a well-articulated philosophy, mission

and goal statement throughout the organization. Keep people informed. Clearly explain what comes next and who's responsible for what. Allow for open and free discussion regardless of each person's position within the organization.Individuals and groups need to understand the broader organizational strategy in order to stay focused and committed to the implementation and adoption of the new strategy. Results of their efforts should be shared throughout the organization. The plan must be executed rapidly and fluidly for it to be relevant. The value in strategic planning is only realized through successful implementation. However, it's during implementation that most strategic plans fail. Strategy execution is the systematic implementation of a strategy.The original meaning of the word "execution" was an action of carrying something out. Once desired outcomes are achieved, you continue affirming these actions. This also requires humility. Many leaders recognize the issues and try to fix them without recognizing their own role in sustaining problems. Realism is needed for a good balance.

5 **Strategy Evaluation** is where ongoing refinement and evaluation of performance, culture, communications and other strategic management issues occurs. **Make strategy a part of your culture.** Review the strategic plan with the entire executive team as often as monthly or weekly. This is a critical step to ensure that timelines are met and action plans are carried out. Pivot and tweak the plans throughout the year. Discard the ones that aren't working and double down on the ones that are.

Turbulent Times

Okay, so you've defined your business properly, and you have the right assets and resources to face the changing world. Everyone in the organization is on board with the new plan, and you set to work hammering out the tactics that will bring these new strategies to life. So now, all you have to do is focus on expanding the strategic plan. "Incorrect!" The traditional linear model of strategic planning followed by execution has ceased to be useful. That assumption is flawed. When examining business issues, are you trying to solve a puzzle or a mystery? With enough data and information, you can find the right answer to a puzzle, but no matter how hard you try, it is impossible to find the exact right solution for a mystery. Because of this, a large part of strategy is simply a calculated prediction about what might happen in the future. The pace at which our markets are moving and the pace of technology evolution precludes an ability to even think of having a static long-term strategy. Sometimes, it can mean abandoning the current plan and formulating a new plan altogether. Your strategic plan should not be cast in stone. Good strategic plans are fluid and not rigid. They allow you to adjust to changes in the marketplace. Don't be afraid to change your plan as necessary. The ability to be adaptable and flexible is compulsory in strategic planning.

"The slowdown in China and other emerging economies, the plummeting price of oil, the digital transformation, the imminent incorporation of generation Z into the workforce, the impact of the terrorist threat on the economy, the uncertainty of European politics, the instability of the financial system, rising corruption, and the expiry of business governance models. Thanks to all these factors, the present context is so

uncertain, tumultuous, and fast-paced that a strategic decision cannot survive for very long." —*Paolo Morgado*

There is really no magic to success. All it takes is an engaged team, creative research, scrupulous development, testing to improve ideas, and impeccable execution. Strategic leaders don't settle for today's achievement. They are regularly anticipating needs and preparing new goals for tomorrow. That outlook always places these leaders one step ahead of others.

SECTION THREE

LEADERSHIP PITFALLS

CHAPTER TEN

A TALE OF TWO LEADERS

Many Years ago, English author, Charles Dickens, wrote a book called "A Tale of Two Cities." Those two cities were London and Paris. In a sense, it could be said that the leadership is also a tale of two leaders. The Good versus The Bad.

The London newspaper headline read: "Woman dead in flat for three years: skeleton of Joyce found on sofa with telly still on, Joyce Carol Vincent: How could this young woman lie dead and undiscovered for almost three years?" Dead for three years in a London apartment, and no one missed her? No one called to check on her? How could this have happened, especially in an era of almost limitless communication?

When the story first broke, it made international news, though people in London were especially stunned. How could she have been dead for so long and no one knew about it? Yet, without making **meaningful connections**, we are all doomed to the same oblivion as this poor woman.

In writing classes, students are taught the importance of a good ending to their pieces. Particularly in fiction, where the story is made up, the writer needs to bring the end to a satisfactory close. Even in factual stories, a good ending is important. But what about life itself lived not in the pages of a book or in a movie script, but in flesh and blood? What about our own stories? What kind of finales do they have? How do they wind up? Are the loose ends woven together nicely as in a good piece of writing? Oftentimes, children's stories end with the line, "And they lived happily ever after." In some languages, it's almost a cliché. The whole idea is that whatever the drama- an evil king, a kidnapped princess, a hungry wolf, -the hero or heroine triumphs in the end.

Russian author, Ivan Turgenev, in his story, *Fathers and Sons*, put these words in the mouth of a character: "The life of each of us hangs by a thread, an abyss may gape beneath us any minute, and yet, we go out of our way to cook up all sorts of trouble for ourselves and mess up our lives."—*Fathers and Sons* (New York, NY: Signet Classics, 2005)

Larry and Joseph (not their real names) were brothers, separated by two years, who grew up together in a suburban neighbourhood. Both applied themselves diligently to their studies, did well, and after graduating from high school, went to a university to study business. Both held executive positions with different investment companies.

To some degree (a great degree actually), we are all products of our environment. Though heredity plays a big role, the values we hold come to us from what is around us — our home, our education, our culture. From infancy, we are impacted by what we see and hear. Unfortunately sometimes, we turn away from what we have been taught because we think we can achieve a greater reward by doing it our way.

Today, in their mid-sixties, Larry lives in a nursing home while Joseph lives comfortably surrounded by loved ones.

Larry chose profit over people.

Joseph chose people over profit.

Larry's story was a story of power politics, manipulation, misguided loyalty, jealousy, and deceit. He clawed, trampled, and manipulated his way to the top. Power struggles come in various forms. Whether over the rule of empires, over companies, or nations, the fight for control can be ugly. Larry didn't care about anyone but himself. He worked long hours and expected others to do so. On the surface, he achieved excellent results, but at what cost? When controlled by selfishness and greed, leaders become dispirited, act in unhealthy ways, disregard deeply held values that leads to distrust by their team. When leaders sacrifice too much for too long, they are often cut off from support and relationships with people. Larry's family broke up in the process since he wasn't involved in their lives. The long hours took a toll on him healthwise, as he suffered two heart attacks. The company declared bankruptcy resulting from his unethical practices. Many workers lost their jobs. He served a short stint in prison. His picture is not even displayed in the companies' "Hall of Fame" wall.

There is a story about a man in a boat who began to drill a hole under his feet where he sat. When people in the boat demanded that he stop, he responded: "This is none of your business. This is my place!"This is the logic used by the entangled leader to justify his or her behaviour. This is my life; it has nothing to do with you. Of course, anything we do or don't do has an impact on others, especially on those nearest to us. The consequences of bad choices affect not just ourselves, but our employees, families, and friends. Our influence is so much greater than we imagine. Who hasn't felt, in a big way, the results of other people's actions, either good or bad?

Joseph, on the other hand, took his responsibility for people quite deeply. He led with humility, authenticity, and integrity. He focused on helping his team grow, and sometimes didn't see eye to eye with the Board of Directors because he was more concerned if the new direction would make his people better off. He sincerely cared about people. Although his results met what was expected of him, in the end, Joseph was relinquished of his duties because of his stance. He moved on to another company for a lesser salary and continued to follow the principles and values he was brought up with. Though

Joseph was no longer with that company, his team still today maintain a close relationship with him.

"You are free to make the choices but you are not free to choose the consequences."—Unknown

You reap what you sow. Some potato farmers decided to save the biggest potatoes for themselves and to plant the smaller potatoes as seed. After a few disappointing harvests, they discovered that nature had reduced their potato crops to the size of marbles. Through this disaster, those farmers learned an important law of life. "They could not have the best things in life for themselves and use the leftovers for seed. The law of life decreed that the harvest would reflect the planting. "In another sense, planting small potatoes is still common practice. We take the big things in life for ourselves and plant the leftovers. We expect that by some crazy twist of natural laws, our selfishness will be rewarded with unselfishness."

Both brothers had the same opportunities, the same chances, and the same set of choices. Larry chose one way, Joseph another. Each now is living with the consequences of those choices. Choices—we all have them, we all have to make them, and we all have to live with the consequences of the ones we make. Hence, the important question for us all is: What will those choices be, and how can we know how to make the right ones?

Acouple of years ago, in the United States, a man won the lottery, taking home more than $113 million. Within a few years, his life was destroyed; the money that had become his God also became the thing that led to his ruin.

The ship, Chanunga, on its way from Liverpool to America, had a massive collision with a small vessel from Hamburg. Crowded with more than two hundred passengers, the ship sank a half hour after the crash. The Chanunga's lifesaving boats were lowered in order to reach the shipwrecked persons, but only thirty-four were saved. Why such a small proportion? Almost all had seized their belts of gold and silver and tied them round their waists. Refusing to lose their money, they lost their lives (and their money) instead.

All throughout recorded history, people have sensed that humanity is in some sort of battle; a warfare, a struggle between competing forces. The poet, T. S. Eliot wrote, "In all of my years, one thing does not change. However, you disguise it, this thing does not change: The perpetual struggle of Good and Evil."—T. S. Eliot: The Complete Poems and Plays. In today's world, money and power are often considered the primary motivations for human behaviour; at least, for those consumed by self-interest. Selfish leaders live only in the present; they are concerned only with what they see and with the immediate reward. They think of themselves before others, and will resort to deception and abuse. Their eyes are fixed on the prize of immediate reward.

In 2011, Steve Jobs, the founder of Apple, died. He was 56. Years earlier, after a bout with cancer, Jobs called death the single best invention of life because it forced us to achieve the best we could here. In other words, because our time is so limited, we must try to be as successful as we can now.

Everyone is born, lives, and one day, will die. These are the broad parameters of the plot of life. In between, life consists of many smaller plots that often are motivated by conflict or tension. Every story needs a setting. You create that setting by your actions.

South African, Laurens Van der Post, had a rock sitting on his living room table. When asked about the "strange black stone," he responded that it came from fifteen thousand feet below the surface of Africa. It was sent to him by a friend who, in the accompanying letter, wrote: "This is a symbol of what you and I have tried to build on all our lives." We all build upon foundations. In the most literal sense, we build our lives upon the rocks beneath our feet, but in another, we build our lives around the principles that govern us. Most people govern their lives by fundamental principles while others do not.

The question is how will your story end? Larry destroyed relationships whilst his brother built connections. Joseph is surrounded by loves and enjoys spending time with family and friends. Larry now lays in a nursing home alone and confined to a bed. Sometimes, weeks go by and he has no visitors. His children don't feel obligated to care for him since he never spent much time with them. Additionally, his relationship with his brother, Joseph, was destroyed a long time ago because of his cut-throat tactics.

Using a metal detector purchased from a rummage sale, Englishman Terry Herbert discovered gold-plated Anglo-Saxon weaponry and silver artefacts buried beneath a farmer's field. The estimated monetary value of the find exceeded five million U. S. dollars. Like someone seeking treasure in a field of dirt, rocks, and rubbish, we must be careful not to let things get in our way and make us miss the real treasure. The treasure is people. It's about building and maintaining connections— valuable relationships. You can only leave a lasting legacy in the hearts and minds of people.

Doing the right thing does not necessarily guarantee your story will end well. There are some things we are definitely are not in control of. However, for the most part, our lives area result of the choices we make. Some choices limit future possibilities and opportunities. If you want a better life, make wise choices.

CHAPTER ELEVEN

THE RISE OF TOXIC LEADERSHIP

A **toxic leader** is a person who has responsibility over a group of people or an organization, and who abuses the leader–follower relationship by leaving the group or organization in a worse-off condition than when s/he first found it. The phrase was coined by Marcia Whicker in 1996, and is linked with a number of dysfunctional leadership styles.

Recent decades have seen a plethora of these toxic leaders. Organizations often hire and promote narcissistic leaders who are dedicated to self-interest. It seems that they mistake their ruthless and cunning behaviour for charisma, confidence, and passion. After all, such traits as humility and compassion are of little help in getting noticed as one climbs the corporate ladder. Leaders are driven, competitive, self-confident and smart. This trend is clearly evident also in politics, as evidenced by the popular support for such leaders. Unfortunately, we frequently fail to distinguish between the *principled visions* of non-toxic leaders and the *grand illusions* of their toxic counterparts.

The corporate scandals of the past few years offers a growing list of toxic leaders.Tyco's Dennis Kozlowski, WorldCom's Bernard Ebbers, ImClone's Sam Waksal, and HealthSouth's Richard Scrushy went from corporate giants to convicted criminals injust a few short years.

Sometimes we prefer delusions rather than to face our fears. Hence, we fall into the grasps of toxic leaders. Jeffrey Skilling, former CEO of Enron, predicting a huge spike in the next year's stock price just as the company was collapsing, is but one classic example. Toxic leaders comfort us with reassuring and often impressive illusions that they will produce better-than-ever seen results. The sad truth is that followers enable and abet toxic leaders. Followers who are confronted with toxic leaders unsurprisingly find excuses to tolerate them. Hitler couldn't carry out his plan to annihilate Jews and dictate at the level he did without the help of millions of German voters, workers, and soldiers. Toxic leaders often surround themselves with entourages of **loyalists and sycophants**, people whose power comes from their relationship with the leader and who; therefore, are faithful to the leader at all costs. Employees submit to bad bosses because they want their pay checks or are afraid to lose their jobs.

"They came for the Socialists, and I did not speak out— because I was not a Socialist. Then, they came for the Trade Unionists, and I did not speak out—because I was not a Trade Unionist. Then, they came for the Jews, and I did not speak out—because I was not a Jew. Then, they came for me—and there was no one left to speak for me." —Martin Niemöller

Martin Niemöller (1892–1984) was a prominent Protestant pastor who emerged as an outspoken public foe of Adolf Hitler, and who spent the last seven years of Nazi rule in concentration camps. The quotation above stems from Niemöller's lectures during the early post-war period.

Theo Veldsman, of the University of Johannesburg, recently published a study on the growth and impact of toxic leadership on organizations. He contends that "there is a growing incidence of toxic leadership in organizations across the world." Veldsman says that subjective research indicates that one out of every five leaders is toxic, and he argues that his research shows it is closer to three out of every ten leaders.

A poll conducted back in 2012 by the National Leadership Index (NLI), released by the Center for Public Leadership at Harvard Kennedy School, and Merriman River Group is an annual measurement of public attitudes toward 13 different sectors of American life ranging from business and non-profits to politics and religion.

In the last 20 years, 30% of Fortune 500 chief executives have lasted less than three years. Top executive failure rates are as high as 75%, and rarely less than 30%. Chief executives now are lasting 7.6 years on a global average - down from 9.5 years in 1995. According to the Center for Creative Leadership, 38% new chief executives fail in their first 18 months on the job.

According to PwC's CEO Success Study, *"CEO turnover at the 2500 largest companies in the world rose from 14.3% in 2014 to 16.6% in 2015—a record high for the CEO Success study."*

Over my career, I have worked for many toxic leaders:

Traits of Toxic Leaders:

1. **The focus is only on what employees are doing wrong**, and rarely gives positive feedback for what they're doing right. They play to the basest fears and needs of the followers.

2. **Micromanagement**. Processes are so constricting that it makes it nearly impossible for anyone to be inspired or come up with new ideas.

3. **Little or no concern for work/life balance**. It's all about the bottom line; the focus is only on profits, beating the competition, and cost-cutting procedures.

4. **They rule by manipulation**. They are egotistical. They talk down to employees and openly criticize them. Toxic leaders exploit their followers' psychological desires and fears. Those who fail to comply with the leader or question the leader's actions are disciplined.

5 **They take credit for others' work**. They are only concerned about looking good; creating a good impression.

6 **Lack of integrity and honesty**. They would do almost anything to maintain their public image.

7 **Low employee morale**. High levels of turnover and absenteeism.

Crisis may also gave rise to toxic leaders. Albert J. Dunlap took over as CEO of Sunbeam Corporation, a maker of small appliances, in 1996. He was best known as a turnaround specialist and professional downsizer who employed ruthless methods to streamline failing companies. Just imagine, he began his tenure at Sunbeam by screaming at the executive team. He was rude and arrogant. Under his reign team spirit and employee morale was at an all-time low. The company ultimately disintegrated into bankruptcy. His widespread layoffs and fraudulent earnings have put him on several lists of worst CEOs.

According to a 2010 survey conducted by the Workplace Bullying Institute, 35 percent of the American workforce has directly experienced bullying—or "repeated mistreatment by one or more employees that takes the form of verbal abuse, threats, intimidation, humiliation, or sabotage of work performance"—while an additional 15 percent said they have witnessed bullying at work. Approximately 72 percent of those bullies are bosses.

Toxic leaders sap the strength out of their organizations. In this demoralizing and dehumanizing atmosphere, employees function out of fear. Toxic leaders are often extreme narcissists.

Tomas Chamorrow-Premuzic has pondered the question of **"Why We Love Narcissists."** He argues that narcissists; however productive some may be, "have parasitic effects on society." He says, "When in charge of companies, they commit fraud, demoralize employees, and devalue stock. When in charge of countries, they increase poverty, violence, and death rates."

WHAT CAN THE ORGANIZATION DO?

1. **Transparency in the selection processes**. Those responsible for hiring senior executives need to give more weight to the attributes that constitutes good leadership such as integrity, authenticity, empathy, and humility.

2. **Well-developed Psychometric assessments** of leadership candidates should be part of the recruitment and interview process to expose narcissistic personalities.

3. A **longer probationary period needs to be in place for new hires.** This will allow time for them to reveal their true agenda.

4. **Protective mechanisms for whistle-blowers**. A whistle-blower protection system needs to be established, so that employees who have witnessed or been a victim of their vicious behaviour can feel secure when coming forward with information.

5. **Periodic 360 degree reviews of individual leaders**. Confidential reviews of leaders by those with whom they interact frequently would go far toward giving

those leaders a clear perspective on their strengths and weaknesses.

6   **Regular accountability forums.** When leaders are required to hold regular town-hall meetings or other such forums, there is increased tendency that they will think more acutely about the decisions and actions that they have taken or are considering.

7   **Appointment of an employee action team** who handles employee issues, and will have the authority to bypass the accused leader and seek intervention when dealing with such cases.

"The world is a dangerous place to live; not because of the people who are evil, but because of the people who don't do anything about it." — Albert Einstein

WHAT CAN YOU DO?

A follower in that situation can confront the leader. But, they must realize non-compliance will unleash the toxic leader's wrath. They can also try to avoid them. I have personally experienced following the chain of command and making a complaint. However, most of the time, it goes nowhere. Witnesses are scared to come forward, and the toxic leader will then convince others that the real problem is you. That is why it is important to always keep documentation and evidence of events. Once you become a whistle-blower, you enter a terrain loaded with land mines. Do your *due diligence* to know which of the *leader's non peers*, you should approach with this complaint. Once such a leader is informed, you are the spearhead of the revolution, they will not only negatively target you, but also, your close associates in an effort to isolate you. Toxic environments are transmissible. They will infect you and will carry over to your personal life. Nothing is worth the toll that a toxic work environment has on your health and well-being. If you hit a dead end, leaving is also an honourable strategy, particularly when you are convinced that neither you nor your collaborators can prevail or that the toxic impact is limited solely to you. When leaving is the only way to preserve your integrity and/or your mental or physical health, it's probably time to go. I choose freedom. In my situation, I planned carefully an exit strategy. Remember to integrate financial and family costs into the calculus. Then, when the time was right, I gracefully resigned.

Our world needs Wise Leaders:

⮑ **The wise listen intuitively**. They speak humbly. Their silent reflection is motivated by a lack of arrogant self-assurance. The wise give consideration to the other person's ideas; therefore, the wise will take time to think through and weigh the evidence. They practice intuitive listening. This is crucial to gaining a complete understanding of situations. Without this full understanding, one can easily waste everyone's time by solving the wrong problem or merely addressing a symptom, not the root cause. The skill of intuitive listening is the heartbeat of all communication. Great leaders function at this level. They listen beyond what is being said; the hidden meaning. They read between the lines. By practicing the skill of intuitive listening, leaders can make better decisions, build stronger relationships, and resolve problems more quickly.

THE THREE LEVELS OF LISTENING

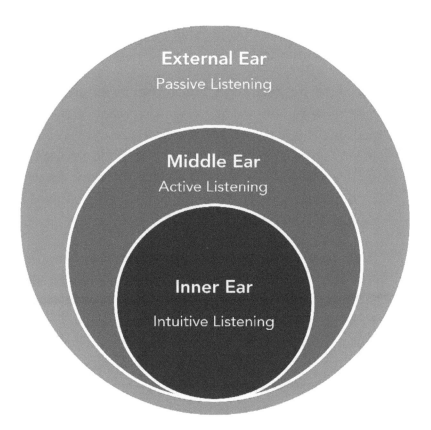

External Ear
Passive Listening

Middle Ear
Active Listening

Inner Ear
Intuitive Listening

➲ **The wise value learning and knowledge.** It is difficult for the foolish to learn because it is hard for them to sit at the feet of a teacher. In contrast, it is easy for the wise to learn because of their humility. They will; thus, enjoy the experience of learning and growing. It is also this search for wisdom and for knowledge that they do not have, which makes them wise.

➲ **The wise are cautious.** The wise are carefully ponder what path they take. They possess good foresight, discernment, and judgement. They will not only trust feelings or personal opinions, they will check things out and ask for advice. Yet, they will always be careful about what other people say to them; they will sort out the good from the bad.

⊃ **The wise possess high Emotional Intelligence**. *They control their emotions.* The wise can remain calm because they do not rely on their own ways. They are not irrational and hot tempered. They don't react, but rather, respond. They build others up. They are aware of their emotions and those of others and harness this for the overall good.

⊃ **They are compassionate and patient**. *They have empathy. Empathy* plays a critical role in one's ability to be a successful leader. Empathy allows leaders to develop and maintain relationships with those they lead. Leaders that possess this trait always make time for people. Many organizations are focused on achieving goals no matter what the cost to employees. Great leaders are concerned about getting the job done, as well as the well-being of those under their care. They are supportive of their employees' development.

"Nobody cares how much you know until they know how much you care". —Theodore Roosevelt

The popularity of toxic leaders in our political, business, and social organizations has become problematic. Toxic leadership is a costly phenomenon. It destroys individuals, organizations and even countries. Failing to purposefully deal with the complex forces that raise our submission to toxic leaders will only promote the devastation that such leaders produce.

CHAPTER TWELVE

Too Many Cooks in the Corporate Kitchen

When "wild in the woods, the savage ran" the art of cookery was not much better understood than the art of painting, but as civilization advanced, the sense of taste developed, as well as our other senses (as nature intended), and the cook came into existence. —Pears' Dictionary of Cookery

There is a popular saying that, "Too many cooks spoil the broth." The same applies to the corporate world.

Here are four reasons there may be too many cooks in the corporate kitchen:

1. **Family Businesses:** Family members have significant stock or ownership in the *company*.

2. **The Marionette Trap:** When an individual is assigned to a position and has to keep his allegiance to those who appointed him (many advisors).

3. **Mergers & Acquisitions**: Poor governance resulting in lack of clarity as to who decides what; both the acquirer and acquiree are involved in the decision making process.

4. **Democratic Leadership**: If this leadership style is practiced by weak leaders, others may overstep their bounds. Also, **unqualified individuals** who are selected for a position may be overly dependent on the expertise and experience of others.

"No one is born a great cook. One learns by doing." —Julia Child

So, how do you know when there are too many cooks in the corporate kitchen?

1. **Low Customer Satisfaction:** Consumers don't find your product satisfying. There are too many ingredients

mixed into one dish; therefore, the product is not differentiated. You have not segmented the market by catering to different consumer tastes, and you may end up with a product that lacks flavour, is overcooked, salty, or spicy. When you try to appeal to everyone, you end up emotionally appealing to no one. Instead of a high-quality product, your product is basic, watered down, and stripped of features customers prefer. There is quantity over quality. Your concoctions have become unpalatable. When consumers aren't getting what they what, then it's easy for them to transition to the competition. Competitors will happily open their doors and add the dessert as a complimentary offer on the menu.

"I don't consider myself a rock star chef, I really don't. I cook for a living and I try to help out as many people as I can in my life, and that's all I care about. I don't care about the fame of television, I use to a lot." —Robert Irvine

2 **Poor Communication:** No one is taking the time to listen. This may lead to freezing marketing or chopping product development. Head chefs are out of touch with reality, (customer needs) focusing more on their abilities and food preparation skills. Each chef advises employees differently concerning policies. Messages frequently lack relevance to their audience, and employees don't know where they fit in to the big picture. Employees are left confused and are not sure of the overall strategy. By adding too many ingredients, (responsibilities, directives, etc.), staff can become overwhelmed and eventually become burned

out, which tends to lead to a decline in employee engagement and high staff turnover. If you continually change the recipe (responsibilities, company initiatives, etc), staff can become confused, disoriented, and unfocused, which tends to lead to a decline in employee engagement and high staff turnover. These scenarios can cause severe damage to the organization. It's time to peel away obstacles, blend chunks of messages into bite-sized bits, and paste proper channels of communications suitable for the type of message to be conveyed.

"To get the customer experience right, you must first get the employee experience right."—Unknown

3   **Internal Conflict:** Have you ever been in a kitchen restaurant during peak time? Pots are sizzling, appliances are whistling, and there is chaos in the kitchen. The temperature is high and the pressure is on, as the shareholders and board of directors are waiting for you to deliver. Essentially, what occurs is that numerous individuals want to be in the position to offer insight, decide the direction of the business, and participate in the formation of the strategy. A combative atmosphere exists amongst the chefs. It has become a frenetic culinary battle, as conflict erupts and each individual blames someone else for spoiling the stew.

4   **Indigestible Meetings:** Multiple lengthy meetings to brainstorm and sift through options. There are more options, which means more possibilities, but it also means decision fatigue. The fewer people that are involved in negotiation, the easier it is to get people

to agree. Too many choices exhaust us and reduce our ability to make a shrewd choice. Researcher, Barry Schwartz calls this **"choice overload."** "As the number of options increases, the costs in time and effort of gathering the information needed to make a good choice also increase," writes Schwartz. "The level of certainty people have about their choice decreases, and the anticipation that they will regret their choice increases."

5. Failure: Here, you invite the food critics to roast you. The project has gone sour (too many onions), completely spoilt, and your time seems to be up. You just can't sugar-coat the results; it's noticeably smoked, dry, and unappetizing. The strategy was poorly executed, as each chef keeps coming up with new ideas; therefore, adding the ingredient he / she thinks is needed to

make a fine cuisine. Decisions weren't left to marinate before moving to the next. Thyme is the base essence of any decision. There is a lack of economies of scale, as efforts are not properly coordinated. No one checks with one another before throwing in ingredients. There is not enough monitoring and control. Expenditure overspill (increases) due to failed projects, as well as costly rework. "Failure has no friends" — John F. Kennedy. All eyes are on you; you are responsible for the outcome. You may be sweating, but you have to stand the heat and provide detailed explanations and answers to questions of what went wrong. Don't sink into despair. You may feel deflated or whipped, but more than ever, you need to get it together and go back to the drawing board. If the food was burnt, it's no use crying over spilled milk.Get the recipe book and use careful analysis and planning to calculate the path forward.

"Pleasure in the job puts perfection in the work." — *Aristotle*

The increasingly crowded corporate kitchen has never been in greater need of one recognised Head Chef who takes the knife and **carves** the strategy and the framework in which others operate.The leader will have to learn how to put his / her foot down and say, "Enough!" (Come to a decision). There can only be one Head Chef; the rest may be assistant chefs who have expertise in different culinary styles. *The vision must be alluringly garnished and mesmerizing. Roles must be refreshed; properly clarified to determine who is responsible for adding each ingredient.* A weighted scale should be used to clearly define parameters for how to balance boundaries to optimize communication, so that no one person or department feels out of the loop.

At best, there should be a system in place to evaluate which tasks should be decided by an individual versus a group. More effort should be placed on improving the internal communication between teams, add yeast and knead to make as smooth and flexible as possible. When there are customers to be served, the kitchen must be well organized, emanating a sweet aroma, and communication should be optimal with everyone focused and following the Head Chef's **recipe for success**. "Bon appétit!" Thus, delivering an exquisite gourmet feast that will tantalize customers' taste buds and leave them coming back for more and more! "Mmmm! Magnifique! C'est délicieux."

CHAPTER THIRTEEN

Seven Things Women shouldn't do if they want to be a Top Leader

Human rights is a topic of much discussion. From the Magna Carta (1215) to the French Declaration of the Rights of Man and of the Citizen (1789) to various United Nations declarations, the idea is promoted that human beings possess certain "inalienable rights"; rights that no one can rightfully take away from us. They are ours by virtue of being human (at least that's how the theory goes).

The questions remain: What are these rights? How are we to determine what they are? Can these rights change and, if so, how so? Why should we, as humans, have these rights anyway?

In some countries, women were not given the "right" to vote until the twentieth century (some nations still deny it). In some cultures, women are not allowed to work or hold leadership positions. Although, our current era has the highest-to-date level of acceptance of women leaders in society,there is still an obvious gender gap. Statistics in the S&P 500 companies show that women comprise 44 percent of the total workforce on average, yet only 25 percent of the senior leader roles. The number of women leaders drops significantly in technology, science, and industrial service industries.

Research supports the fact that women have the ability to make better directors than men, and that their presence on corporate boards has been linked to greater organisational performance. One study confirms that boards with high female representation experience a 53 percent higher return on equity, a 66 percent higher return on invested capital, and a 42 percent higher return on sales. Another study demonstrates that by having just one female director on the board cuts the risk of bankruptcy by 20 percent, and other studies have shown that when women directors are appointed, boards adopt new governance practices.

As McMasters University researchers, Chris Bart, and Gregory McQueen point out, there is a strong business case for putting more women on boards. "The correlation between the presence of female board members and corporate performance demonstrates that having women on the board is no longer just the right thing to do based on gender equality arguments, but also, the smart thing to do," says Bart. "More specifically, our research has found that women on boards are significantly better than men at making decisions because of their 'Complex Moral Reasoning' (CMR) abilities. CMR involves acknowledging and considering the rights of others in the pursuit of fairness by using a social cooperation and consensus building approaches that are consistently applied in a non-arbitrary fashion. The dramatic importance of this is highlighted when one considers that the role of directors is solely to make decisions or, more precisely, to help the board make decisions."

If your desire is to be a top leader and to be your best professional self, here are seven things you shouldn't be doing:

1 Unduly Apologizing

Don't believe you need to be quiet or less visible to make your intimidated male counterparts feel more comfortable. Stand tall and refuse to shrink in order to enhance another's sense of importance. Indeed, not everyone will like you, and you are definitely not in a leadership position to win "miss congeniality." Stop unnecessarily apologizing. Leaders must be confident. If you keep second-guessing yourself or are overly concerned about the opinion of others, you are not ready to fully take the reins.

"Women shouldn't feel the need to apologize for who they are and the skills they bring to the table. Confidence and embracing being women rather than apologizing for being women is what will help women rise to the next level and climb the corporate ladder."
—*Sabrina Parsons*

2 Adopting a Persona That You Think is Necessary to Achieve Success

The Wall Street Journal posted an article on September 28 2016, about how *"women may get further ahead professionally if they mask their gender initially"* If you listen to John Greathouse, a leadership expert, he'll advise you to, "create an online presence that obscures your gender." Don't put your full name, use your initials instead. "A gender-neutral persona allows women to access opportunities that might otherwise be closed to them." He goes on to close out his article with "Much like a book, people cannot avoid judging their fellow humans by their "cover." As such, a neutral online persona will encourage more people to evaluate your work products and experience based on inherent qualities, not unclouded preconceptions. After a massive backlash, he later apologized for his role in telling women to endure the gender bias problem instead of acting to help fix it.

Don't try to be someone you are not. It's important to be you. Don't be afraid to share your unique perspective while being true to yourself. Your female view is an additive, and you have an opportunity to evocatively contribute to your company's vision and goals. It's okay to show emotion and be vulnerable. You don't have to be bossy or wear a tough image to be a leader. You can show empathy without being too sentimental. Be yourself. Authenticity acts as a catalyst that earns the respect of followers. Authenticity is critical when directing others since it builds trust.

"It is imperative that women in leadership maintain their intrinsic style while not being afraid to stand their ground when they know they have the best idea or right path forward" —Madison Cork

Yahoo's CEO, Marissa Mayer famously took two weeks of maternity leave in 2012. Many women were outraged. To compensate, she paid to have a *nursery* built in her *office*. We may not fully understand the demands of her job, but it unfortunately creates the false sense that maternity leave is a fallacy. Women in general will internalize the message that if you really want to get ahead and stay at the top of your game, taking advantage of your company's leave policies is not acceptable. True leadership is setting a good example that will have a lasting positive effect in the long run.

A 2007 review by the Organization for Economic Co-operation and Development concluded: Women who make full use of their maternity or parental leave entitlements receive, on average, lower wages in the years following their resumption of work."Mayer's announcement is disappointing," said Anne Weisberg, senior vice-president of the Families and Work Institute in New York. "She's a role model and I think she should take whatever Yahoo's parental leave is – the mark of a great leader is that they have a strong team and don't need to be there all the time themselves. And, she's having twins – just physically, that's a big deal."

3 Overly Embracing the Democratic Leadership Style

Sometimes, the need to fit in can cause women to always collaborate. Participation in decision encourages diverse opinions, helps a leader make better informed decisions, and fosters employee commitment. However, if you keep depending on or continuously seeking advice from others before you make every decision, you will seem weak. You will have to make some tough decisions on your own. To be a top leader, you must have thick skin. Be assertive and decisive. You can do this job. You have the skills and talent and that is why you were chosen. Believe in yourself and stand firmly.

4 **Being Modest about Your Successes and Achievements**

According to Renee Rottner, Assistant Professor, at the University of California, Santa Barbara's Technology Management Program, "Gender-bias limits us whether we are investors, employers or educators. In studies that reveal gender, but keep the content the **same** –venture pitch, resume, and online course material – women are perceived as less competent than men, even though their performance was identical."

New research shows that not voicing achievements holds women back from achieving the same compensation and job satisfaction as men. A recent report from Catalyst, a non-profit organization focused on increasing opportunities for women in business, looks at whether or not doing "all the right things" will advance a woman's career in the same way that it will a man's career. Their research shows that publicly celebrating and acknowledging successes has more impact on women's compensation and career advancement than directly negotiating for better compensation. It's time to celebrate your successes and achievements. There is a difference between speaking about your accomplishments and boasting. If you do not speak at all about your achievements, people will not be aware of what you have accomplished and may overlook and underestimate you. If you don't promote your abilities and skills, nobody else will. "Tooting your own horn" is not something at which women excel at. Celebrating success seems to be viewed as either uncomfortably egotistical, and that's why many women desist from doing this. Women need to put themselves in the spotlight and celebrate their achievements. It's time to make a concerted effort to acknowledge your professional accomplishments as they happen. Your career may in fact depend on it.

5 Failure to Support Other Women

To get to the top is easier if we work together as a team. It's not about competition or comparing yourself to other women. This is something I have seen a lot in the workforce. If you are comfortable with who you are and have confidence in your abilities, it will be easy for you to embrace, support, and respect other female leaders. Building networks can definitely assist in propelling you to the top. Cultivate as much information as possible from those who have been there and done that. Their advice is priceless and can help to teach you how to handle and overcome issues female leaders commonly face.

6 Neglecting Yourself

Take care of yourself. "I wish I could go back and tell myself, Arianna, your performance will actually improve if you can commit to not only working hard, but also, unplugging, recharging, and renewing yourself." — Arianna Huffington.

Ultimately, your wellbeing is very important to your overall success as a leader. Unless you are healthy, you cannot lead your team with vitality and vigour. It's important to take care of your health;exercise, eat healthy, and get adequate rest. This will help you deal properly with stressful situations. Energy to effectively get the job done comes from a healthy mental and physical state. Only when you take care of yourself can you enjoy the fruits of your leadership.

7 Succumbing to the Narrative about Work-life Balance and Assuming you can't Have a Family and a Career

It is not wise to define success solely in terms of business and work. Sometimes, women may try to overcompensate and may hold back on making personal family decisions. Say "yes" to your goals, and honour yourself and wishes in the process. Don't give up on something you want for a short-term gain. Yes, you can have your cake and eat it. If you need advice in balancing both, seek out mentors and supportive groups. I have met many women who wished they could go back and change the hands of time, but unfortunately, they can't. Yes, accomplishing the organization's goals is important, but what about your personal goals?

If you want to go to the top, you must be confident and believe in yourself. Yes, the gender issue does exist, but that is not the main consideration. You should focus on making a valuable contribution; taking care of your employees and yourself and leaving a positive legacy.

SECTION FOUR

SUSTAINING THE LEADER WITHIN

CHAPTER FOURTEEN

THE COST OF LEADERSHIP

Society gives high commendation to individuals who lead transformational change, but this, at times, has proven to be a difficult and daunting task. There are but a handful of leaders who can be classified as remarkable. These leaders' pioneered great changes that positively revolutionized our world, but it came at a great cost. Martin Luther King Jr. was assassinated. Mahatma

Ghandi was assassinated. Nelson Mandela was imprisoned. Abraham Lincoln was assassinated. They all came to the point of decision-making and endured "**Crossing the Rubicon.**"

The phrase "**Crossing the Rubicon**" means to pass a point of no return, and refers to Julius Caesar's crossing of the Rubicon River in 49 BC, which was considered an act of insurrection. It refers to any individual or group committing itself irrevocably to a risky or revolutionary course of action. When we make a difficult decision from where there is no way back, we say we *cross the Rubicon*. Julius Caesar uttered the famous phrase "***alea iacta est***"—**the die is cast**—as his army marched through the shallow river.

Most people desire the **glory, power, *and* preferential treatment** that leaders enjoy. Few; however, are willing to pay the price that those leaders paid to get those benefits. Leadership is expensive; it is costly. Are you ready to pay the price?

PHYSICAL COSTS

The cost of leadership involves discipline. Every impulse, every ambition, and every desire *must* be submitted to achieving the vision. Laziness and leadership does not go hand in hand. It takes blood, sweat, and tears in order to be developed to your fullest leadership potential. You will always be expected to do the work, even when others are unwilling. As leaders, we must remember that we work for others rather than for ourselves, and that we can't expect more of others than we do of ourselves. When training for an event, an athlete puts aside every unhealthy indulgence that would tend to weaken the physical abilities, and by gruelling, persistent discipline, they train their muscles to strength and endurance, so that when the day of the competition should arrive, they push themselves to the maximum limit. They give it their all. Leaders gave it their all to ensure that their vision is realized. Leadership will cost you comfort. You may be moving from place to place. You go where leadership takes you. This can be unnerving for your loved ones. If you are leading well, you don't often get to lead "comfortably".

"Great leaders truly care about those they are privileged to lead and understand that the true cost of the leadership privilege comes at the expense of self-interest." —Simon Sinek

EMOTIONAL COSTS

Being a leader will cost you emotionally. It will never cease to affect you. Leadership is risky. If you are in the front of a battle you are more likely to get hit by a bullet because you are positioned where the ammunition is flying. If you're going to lead, you'd better comprehend the truth. There will always be difficulties along the way. The problems come, and the problems go; walking into leadership means *walking into conflict.* Conflict is not always bad. It can force us to face ourselves and others honestly. But, in the short term, conflict usually drains us emotionally. *Many times, I have found myself at the centre of conflict.* If I had never led, I never would have been at the centre of controversy. It was a risk. Leading is one of the most emotionally draining things you will ever do. You will discover that you can go from the highest of highs to the lowest of lows with one phone call or email. Being in front and walking by yourself can sometimes feel lonely. Leading may also mean experiencing times of *loneliness.* You may lose friends and family support along the way. Great leaders always put others first, which often results in allotting the majority of our time for the multitude. Friends and family will feel left out as you focus your attention dealing with pertinent issues.

Not everyone will understand and support you and, many times, that means standing on your own. You must believe in yourself and in the journey, and then act confidently upon those beliefs. You will face many obstacles along the path including fear, failure, rejection, and disappointments. Good leadership goes into the unknown and that can be scary. Even the best leaders are anxious at times about what is next. Leaders also risk *failure*. You'll be handling more responsibilities, and sometimes, you will fail.

PERSONAL COSTS

It is a sacrifice. For starters, it will cost you *time*. You have to be willing to put in the effort and the long hours, and deal with the myriad of issues that seem to constantly arise; you might lose yourself. Everyone wants a piece of you. Leaders give up their personal aspirations for the good of others, the team, or the organization. It's not thinking about yourself, but putting the needs of others first. We have to be willing to work the hardest, even when everyone else has dropped out. Everyone is depending on you. What comes out of you must be good. You have to be the best for your followers. Your goal is to make more leaders. The ideology of leadership is that those being led should be better off because of the leader. **It's a great responsibility**. If you fail, the team will fail. That is a lot of weight to be carrying on your shoulders. All eyes are on you, and you are the example. You will always be a leader wherever you go. It's not a cloak you can remove. You will not live like the rest of the world. You are a role model. You are different. You are set apart. You were called to fulfil a purpose. As a leader, especially one who represents many individuals, your personal opinion is not foremost. You must be able and willing to put yourself aside and speak as a representative rather than as an individual. You are acting as an ambassador for a country. The representation of the fishbowl is often used in leadership education. The theory is that leaders reside in a giant fishbowl, working with only a few individuals, but always being observed by others.

As leaders, we have to continuously be careful about our decisions, our words, and our actions, so that we best represent those whom we serve. We are in the public eye therefore we must behave honourably so that we can maintain credibility and authenticity. In today's world and with social media nothing remains hidden for too long. *Behaving unethically can devastate those you lead.* Our decisions carry impact because of the positions of influence in which followers place us. Think of those you serve and do your best to make the greatest positive change for all. Being a leader may also cost you *money. Sometimes, you will have to take funds out of your own pocket to support your cause and help others.*

POPULARITY

Your desire to undertake leadership shouldn't arise from a belief that others will admire you more. Leading well is no guarantee that a leader will be popular. If you are overly concerned with what others think and want them to like you leadership may not be right for you. You will be judged and criticized. You will have to make the hard decisions that may help some and hurt others. Being at the forefront of the multitude makes you a target. Everything you say and do will be analyzed. It is impossible to reach everybody, and it is improbable to be liked and understood by all of those whom we reach. Many people will not take the time to get to know you and your message. Others will default to opposition and actively fight against you for one reason or another. It is important to understand that there will always be naysayers. We must remain vigilant in our struggles and ever diligent in our work. Leaders take people through change. Change is almost never initially popular.

Sadly, to most people, you will never do enough. A common aphorism is that you can't please everybody, and this is very true in leadership. Much is expected of us, but great work can feel inadequate to others when it is all that is produced. Leaders risk *feeling unappreciated*. Sometimes, you may not even get as much as a "Thank You" for all the time and effort you have given to helping people. Many times, great leaders are never acknowledged until they have passed. Only then do we realize the depth of their contributions.

Colonel George Washington Goethals, the man responsible for the completion of the Panama Canal, had stifling problems with the climate and the geography of Central America. Driving rains, incredible heat, and deadly disease were problems that never left his task. But, his biggest challenge was the growing criticism back home from those who predicted he'd never finish the project. The voices of the critics appeared to be the biggest problem of all.

Finally, a colleague asked him, "Aren't you going to answer these critics?"

"In time," answered Geothals. "When?" his partner asked... "When the canal is finished."

As the leader, you are set apart as "the authority". You may also find that others treat you differently after you become a leader. You may succumb to **pride**. Often, leaders rise to places of responsibility because they do things well. In time, they may be tempted to believe they can do no wrong — or that even if they do — things will turn out all right." Leadership is power and absolute power corrupts. Corruption is little more than unfettered egotism. We need *accountability partners* — friends with whom we can be absolutely honest without fear of condemnation, and who will tell us the truth. We need to surround ourselves with the right people. Many people have different motives for following us and it can be selfish or treacherous.

We must be able to decipher what types of followers are in our camp and know whom to keep in our inner circle. The closer someone is to you, the easier it is for them to wound you and this can abruptly end your leadership presence. Many leaders fall because of surrounding themselves with the wrong types of followers. *A good leader knows the importance of followers and is aware of the type of followers he has.* Followers impact leaders and the leadership process.

THE SEVEN TYPES OF FOLLOWERS

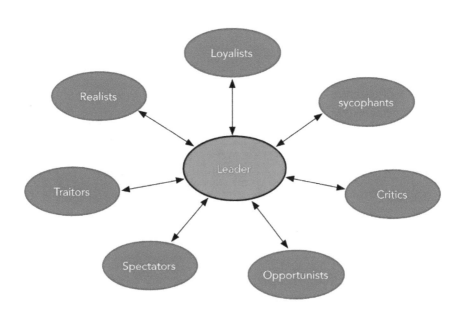

1 **Loyalists** - The **genuine supporters**. They are highly engaged and work hard to support the leader.

2   **Sycophants** - The **flatterers**—"yes people". **Sycophants** are not truthful; (if you say the sky is green, they will say, "yes") and can set the leader up for a great fall. Be wary of them.

3   **Critics** - The **opposition**. The detractor's goal is to challenge and question the leader's every behaviour and policy.

4   **Opportunists** - The **freebooters**. They have a price and can easily be bought. They like to be close to the powerful, and their allegiance is to whoever is on top at the moment.

5   **Spectators** - The **observers**. They are neither here nor there, but just stand on the sidelines. They are disengaged and hold a position of neutrality about the leader.

6   **Traitors** - The **silent haters** and conspirators. They are hard to spot (until it's too late), as they have gained the leader's trust. They have strong, negative emotional feelings about the leader, and secretly work to undermine him/her... the Judases (**"Et tu, Brute?"**).

7   **Realists**-The **constructive critical thinkers.** If they agree with the current course of action, they will back the leader 100 percent. Alternatively, if they disagree, they will challenge the leader, offering constructive alternatives to help the leader and the organization achieve their goals.

As leaders, we should consider whether we are willing to pay the price for good leadership. It's not cheap if you are at a point of decision-making and are deliberating the path forward. Maybe, it's time for you to "**Cross the Rubicon.**" There is no guarantee of a smooth journey, but it's the only route to carve your footprints in stone. "A man leaves all kinds of footprints when he walks through life," says writer, Margaret Lee Runbeck. "A man doesn't think about it, but everywhere he passes, he leaves some kind of mark." Remember these words and do your best to leave behind a great legacy.

CHAPTER FIFTEEN

HEALTHY LEADERSHIP:
Leading From The Inside Out

"A healthy outside starts from the inside." —Robert Urich

I remember one of my managers who would sit at his desk working long hours, sometimes never getting up. He didn't eat on time or sometimes consume any water for the whole work day. Sadly though, it took a toll on him for the worst, and eventually, led to his demise.

Health is the first necessity of leadership;without which, life pleasures and successes would be unattainable. It is of extreme importance that leaders seek to obey the health laws if they want to perform at an optimum level. Many leaders on the pinnacle of success have had to abruptly retire or resign due to ailing health, which could have been avoided by adopting good lifestyle choices.

Our health is a precious gift. Too little attention is generally given to the preservation of health. It is far better to prevent disease that to know how to treat it when contracted. The responsible caring for our own health brings blessings not only to ourselves, but to those with whom we share our lives. Society pays directly or indirectly for every person's poor health choices. It is important to invest not only in your own health, but also, in the health of your team.

Remember to always consult with your physician or other qualified health care provider before embarking on a new treatment, diet, or fitness program.

WATER

ARE YOU DRINKING ENOUGH WATER?

Our bodies are made up of about 60 percent water. According to a study performed by H.H. Mitchell, published in the Journal of Biological Chemistry, the brain and heart are composed of 73% water, and the lungs are about 83% water. The skin contains 64% water, muscles and kidneys are 79%, and the bones are around 31%. Water is the foundation to all physical life. We need water in order to survive and every cell, tissue, and organ needs water to function. Water increases energy and relieves fatigue. Since your brain is mostly water, drinking it helps you think, focus, concentrate better, and be more alert.

Where exactly is water in the human body? Most of the body's water is in the intracellular fluid (2/3 of the body's water). The other third is in the extracellular fluid (1/3 of the body's water). Water is the primary building block of cells. Water keeps blood flowing throughout the body, helps to regulate body temperature, aids in digestion, transports nutrients and oxygen to the cells. It also cushions joints, boosts the immune system andremoves waste from the body. It can relieve and prevent headaches (migraines & back pains), which are commonly caused by dehydration. Water also promotes weight loss and can put you in a good mood. When the body is functioning at its best, you will feel great and be happy!

According to Dr. Jeffrey Utz, Neuroscience and paediatrics at Allegheny University, different people have different percentages of their bodies made up of water. Babies have the most; being born at about 78%. By one year of age, that amount drops to about 65%. In adult men, about 60% of their bodies are water. However, fat tissue does not have as much water as lean tissue. In adult women, fat makes up more of the body than men, so they have about 55% of their bodies made of water.

An historic experiment conducted by Dr. Pitts at Harvard University had athletes walking on a treadmill at three and a half miles per hour in a hot environment to consume as much water as they lost in their sweat. At the end of the experiment, the athletes felt as if they could continue walking seven hours later!—G.C. Pitts, R.E. Johnson, F.C. Conzolazio, "Work in the Heat as Affected by Intake of Water, Salt, and Glucose," *American Journal of Physiology* 142:253, 1944. The same athletes, deprived of water during the experiment on another day, reached the point of exhaustion within three and half hours.

Insufficient water can impair our vital functions. A chronic water deficiency will lead to poor health. We need to drink more water than our thirst demands. Pure water is superior to other drinks. Start your day with 1-2 glasses of water (you may squeeze a tablespoon of lemon in 1 glass) and continue drinking water between meals to make sure you are well hydrated.

Do you wait until you are thirsty to drink water? Experts recommend 8 (8 oz.) glasses a day or you can take your body weight (in pounds), divide it in half, and drink that many ounces (More when doing strenuous work in hot environments).

Drink water until your urine is pale yellow or colourless. However, don't overdo it. In 2007, newscasts were filled with the tragic news of the unnecessary death of a young woman who died from drinking too much water! Water? Yes. As part of a radio contest, she drank an excessive amount of water and died later that day from water intoxication. Water, although essential for life and usually harmless, can kill when taken in excess.

NUTRITION

The Greek Philosopher, Ludwig Feuerbach, stated that "man is what he eats." Though we certainly are more than what we eat, what we eat helps make us what we are. A healthy diet may improve or maintain optimal health. Our blood, bones, fat, and tissues all are fed by the food we put in our bodies. Food impacts our physical being in many ways. Diet can impact our thoughts since our brain is central to thought, and our brain is affected by the foods that feed it.

It's important to consume a balanced diet. A balanced diet means that you are combining the right fats, proteins, carbohydrates, vitamins, minerals, and fibre in order to obtain all of the nutrients you need for good health. By eating the correct combination, you will give your body the right fuel to grow, replenish, repair, and strengthen. The goal of good nutrition is to choose foods that promote good health, prevent disease, and help us to live long, productive lives.

MYPLATE FOOD GUIDE

The U.S. Department of Agriculture (USDA) stopped using the Food Pyramid in June 2011 (ending 19 years of USDA food pyramid diagrams). **MyPlate** is the current nutrition guide. The MyPlate logo divides a dinner plate into four sections for vegetables, fruits, grains, and proteins with a fifth smaller plate to one side for dairy. Using an image of a plate helps with basic meal planning and understanding the general concepts of balance.

FOOD GROUPS:

- **Grains** includes oatmeal, brown rice and grain products such as breads, pasta and crackers; Starchy vegetables, including all varieties of potatoes, squash, and corn. Make at least half your grains whole grains. Choose brown rice in place of white rice and whole-wheat breads and whole-grain pasta whenever possible.

- **Dairy.** Examples of dairy products include milk, butter, yoghurt, cheese. It is better to switch to fat-free or low-fat (1%) milk. The categorization of dairy as a food group with recommended daily servings has been criticized by, for example, the Harvard School of Public Health points out that "research has shown little benefit, and considerable potential for harm, of such high dairy intakes. Moderate consumption of milk or other dairy products—one to two servings a day—is fine, and likely has some benefits for children. But it's not essential for adults, for a host of reasons."

⊃ **Protein**. All foods made from meat, poultry, seafood, eggs, legumes including beans and peas, processed soy products, nuts and seeds are considered part of the protein food group. These foods are all good sources of protein, which is essential for the body to grow and repair itself. Legumes are a good alternative to meat dishes. They are the richest in protein of all plant foods and are high in fibre. If you do consume meat, it is better to choose lean protein.

⊃ **Fruits** includes apples, oranges, bananas, berries and lemons among others. 100% fruit juice also counts as part of this food group. Fruits are good sources of many essential nutrients that are underconsumed, including potassium, dietary fibre, vitamin C, and folate (folic acid).

⊃ **Vegetables** refers to all vegetables. This would include lettuce, carrots, tomatoes, broccoli, cabbage, etc.; all vegetables except starchy vegetables.

Fats and Oils are not a food group, but they provide essential nutrients and are therefore included in USDA food patterns. Use sparingly. Limit your solid fat intake and make sure that most of your fat sources come from fish, nuts and vegetable oils.

HOW MUCH SHOULD OUR DAILY INTAKE FROM EACH FOOD GROUP BE?

Eat the right amount of calories for you based on your age, sex, height, weight, and physical activity level. Eating well is all about balancing your nutritional needs to meet your health goals.

There's something in fruits and vegetables that makes us live longer and better.It is best to eat plant-based foods rather than processed foods. Make half your plate fruits and vegetables. Fruit and vegetables are a vital source of vitamins and minerals. There's evidence that people who eat at least five portions a day have a lower risk of heart disease, stroke and some cancers. Have a mixture of different colours of food as they are rich in antioxidants and phytochemicals provide vitamins and minerals.

Eat less saturated fat, sugar, and salt. Avoid fried foods and cooking with oil. Too much saturated fat can increase the amount of cholesterol in the blood, which increases your risk of developing heart disease. Avoid artificial sweeteners. Frequently consuming foods and drinks high in sugar increases your risk of obesity and diabetes. Drink water instead of sugary drinks. Additionally, if you eat too much salt, it can raise your blood pressure. The higher your blood pressure, the greater the strain on your arteries, brain, kidneys and heart. This can lead to strokes, heart attacks and kidney disease.

If you must eat between meals use fruits and nuts as healthy snacks. Nuts are high in fibre but they do still contain high levels of fat, so eat them in moderation. Choose unsalted nuts and seeds to keep sodium intake low.

Avoid junk food; it comes laden with excess calories, fat and salt, that aid in the emergence of chronic diseases. Try to incorporate fresh salads with your meals. Limit consumption of condiments and spices. They are stimulating to the body, but can weary the brain and nerves, increase heart rate, deplete iron and also cause acid reflux and indigestion. Therefore avoidor reduce consumption of vinegar foods, ketchup, mustard, salad dressings, pickles and black and white pepper, etc.

ARE THE COLOURS OF FOODS IMPORTANT?

Whites in foods as cauliflower and garlic, have allicin, which controls blood pressure, cleanses the blood from fat deposits, eliminates harmful substances and has strong anti-inflammatory properties. **Yellow or Orange** foods, such as oranges and carrots contain beta-carotene (a precursor of vitamin A is necessary for the healthy skin, aids in eye health and boosts the immune system. Those with **Red** colour such as tomatoes and watermelon are loaded with powerful, healthy antioxidants as lycopene, an anti-carcinogenic that protects us from cancer. Most **Green** foods, such as spinach and broccoli, are considered super foods because they are rich in lutein and sulforaphane. These reduce the risk of *cardiovascular disease and* many cancers, improve the metabolism of fats and help detoxify the body. It's a scientifically-proven fact that the darker the food, the higher the antioxidant level. **Purple** foods suchas eggplant and cabbage prevent aging and the emergence of degenerative diseases among many.

CAN WHAT YOU EAT AFFECT YOUR MENTAL HEALTH?

In the past ten years, research on the effect of diet and nutrition on mental health has increase rapidly, with mounting evidence validating that diet and nutrition are as important to, as they are to cardiology. Research suggests that fruit and vegetable consumption may be associated with reduced psychological distress. Felice Jacka, president of the International Society for Nutritional Psychiatry Research said, "A very large body of evidence now exists that suggests diet is as important to mental health as it is to physical health. A healthy diet is protective and an unhealthy diet is a risk factor for depression and anxiety,"

Enjoy your food, but remember in diet, temperance is important. Temperance can be difficult in a world that regards excess as success. In general, eat a wide variety of healthy food to meet your nutritional needs while, at the same time, not overeating and taxing the system. Avoid oversized portions. As with everything in health, balance is the key. You could be consuming a balanced diet, and yet, at the same time, be consuming too much fat, salt or sugar; all of which can lead to a variety of serious health issues.

DON'T SKIP BREAKFAST

How many times have I heard, "I am so busy, I'll skip breakfast." Breakfast is the most important meal of the day. Even so, 31 million Americans skip breakfast each morning because they aren't hungry, they don't feel like eating, or they are too busy.

Research shows that eating a breakfast prior to 11 a.m. provides a number of benefits including a reduced risk of heart disease, type 2 diabetes and weight gain, as well as increased physical activity and improved mental abilities.

Start your day off with a healthy breakfast and try not skip meals in spite of how busy your schedule may be.

EXERCISE

A sedentary lifestyle is a direct route to an early grave. It sounds harsh, but it's true. Everyone knows that exercise and nutrition is vital to maintaining health, yet many leaders continue to lead sedentary lives. Absence of muscle contraction during long, uninterrupted stretches of inactivity increases the chances of chronic diseases. Adopting a healthy lifestyle is one of the most important factors to leadership longevity.

"Two-thirds of all illness is the result of our lifestyle choices," says Dr. Edward Phillips, founder of the Institute of Lifestyle Medicine at Harvard Medical School.

When exercise is regularly performed and accompanied with a balanced diet, there is a decreased incidence of lifestyle illnesses. Exercise improves both the strength and the efficiency of your cardiovascular system to get the oxygen and nutrients to your muscles. It keeps muscles strong, and joints, tendons, and ligaments flexible, allowing you to move more easily. It can help you to maintain a healthy weight. The more you exercise, the more calories you burn. In addition, the more muscle you develop, the higher your metabolic rate becomes, so you burn more calories even when you're not exercising. Exercise enhances your immune system and can help prevent the onset of some diseases. Exercise improves brain function. It reduces LDL cholesterol —the type that clogs your arteries, increases HDL —the good cholesterol), and reduces blood pressure, so it lowers the stress on your heart.

"Take care of your body. It's the only place you have to live." —*Jim Rohn*

Exercise also increases blood flow and oxygen levels in the brain. It encourages the release of the brain chemicals that are responsible for the production of cells in the hippocampus; the part of the brain that controls memory and learning. Exercise can also help you sleep better. Physical activity stimulates the release of endorphins, which make you feel better and more relaxed; these, in turn, improve your mood. People who exercise regularly have less depression. Exercise plays a role in the prevention of breast and colon cancer. The benefits of exercise are many and varied.

Before starting an exercise program; however, you need to be sure that your health will permit regular exercise. If there are any pre-existing health conditions or disabilities, it is wise to be guided by a physician as to the appropriate intensity of exercise to be undertaken. **Get Medical Clearance from your doctor first!**

Three points need to be kept in mind with any exercise program: frequency, intensity, and duration:

1. **Frequency:** Current guidelines from the American Heart Association call for 150 minutes of moderate physical activity per week or about 30 minutes of exercise five times a week.

2. **Intensity:** The appropriate intensity of exercise will vary depending upon your age, weight goals, and medical condition. Over time, if you are consistent, you will be able to increase the intensity of your workout. For exercise to be effective, it's good to get your heart beating faster and to work up a sweat, but go at your own pace. Listen to your body.

3. **Duration:** It would be beneficial if exercise were at least done for 30 minutes, five days per week. The exercise time may be divided into portions;three days per week —cardio and two days per week— strength training. It should be arranged to suit your goals. If you are now beginning, starting off slow. Walking is an excellent and sustainable form of exercise.

A well-rounded fitness program includes **aerobic exercise, resistance training,** and **flexibility and balance exercises**:

⊃ **Aerobic or Cardiorespiratory** exercise, often abbreviated to "cardio", is any exercise that increases the heartbeat and breathing rate. Such exercises include walking, running, swimming, and cycling. Cardio exercises improve your heart and lung strength. During aerobic exercise, your working muscles demand more oxygen, and this prompts the heart to work harder to increase the volume of blood it can deliver to the muscles. Your lungs; meanwhile, become more efficient in delivering oxygen to the blood and removing the carbon dioxide waste.

⊃ **Resistance training,** also called strength training or weight training is the use of resistance to muscular contraction to build the strength, anaerobic endurance, and size of skeletal muscles. It can be performed with free weights, such as barbells and dumbbells, or by using weight machines. You can also increase your strength through other types of resistance exercises, such as by using your body weight or resistance bands. Resistance training helps to improve joint function, bone density, muscle, and tendon and ligament strength.

⊃ **Flexibility and Balance Exercises:** Activities that lengthen and stretch muscles can help you prevent injuries, back pain, balance problems, and also, improve posture. A well-stretched muscle more easily achieves its full range of motion. **Stretching** can help your body stay limber.

Additionally, varying your workouts can help you push past a training plateau.

Research has also found that people who sit for long periods were 24 percent more likely to die from health problems, as compared with people who sat less. But, exercising for short periods does not completely counteract the risks that come with sitting for a long time. Among studies that looked at cancer type, sitting for too long was associated with a higher risk of being diagnosed with or dying of breast, colon, colorectal, endometrial, or ovarian cancers, the researchers found. Too much sitting can also cause back pain and blood clots to develop. **Sit Less**.

It has been proven that people who exercise have a longer and better life expectancy than those who do not. It's time to take responsibility for your health. It's never too late to start a fitness regimen, and there's no reason to give up existing exercise if you're in good health and your doctor approves of your activity.

REST

"Take rest; a field that has rested gives a bountiful crop." —
Ovid

A bright, young medical student at Loma Linda found himself burning out. Getting up at four in the morning and working until midnight, he struggled to keep up with his strenuous curriculum, but to no avail. He fell further and further behind. "In desperation, he went to his professor for help. Being an astute man, the professor recommended that Tom get at least seven hours of sleep each night, no matter what, and thirty minutes of vigorous exercise every day. Tom was sceptical. . . but at last, he reluctantly agreed to give this program a try. After all, he was so far down he had nothing to lose. To his utter astonishment, his grades began to improve within just two weeks. By the end of the year, he was in the upper third of his class and, in due time, successfully completed his medical training.—"I'm So Tired," Hardinge Lifestyle Series (Loma Linda, Calif.: Loma Linda University School of Health, 1988)

Tom's body needed time to rest. We too need time for daily rest. Continuously depriving your body of much needed sleep produces, in time, physical and emotional harm. No matter how young, how healthy you are our bodies need rest and, sooner or later, an unbalanced lifestyle will catch up to you.

Many of us are just like Tom. We all need to have daily rest, as well as weekly rest in order to achieve optimum health physically, mentally, spiritually, and emotionally.

"I AM SO BUSY"

Many of us live in a very stressed and fast-paced environment filled with so many things to do and so little time. Our schedules are jam packed. Many times, I felt as if I was a headless chicken going in circles. Sadly, the corporate world implies that for you to get ahead, you must sleep less. The more hours you are up, the more opportunity to achieve success. Mother Teresa said, "I think today the world is upside down, and is suffering so much because there is very little love in the home and in family life. We have no time for our children; we have no time for each other. There is no time to enjoy each other."

I have seen so many times among leaders that the drive to make money, to get ahead, or to succeed supersedes everything to the point where they sacrifice their marriages, families, and sadly, their own health. We can all agree that working hard and doing one's best is ideal. We can; however, not let this desire for success totally consume us to the point that it becomes our idol and, as a result, we and the ones we love and care about suffer. Frequently, we hear stories where a father who works all the time, stating that he is doing it "for his family" when, in the end, it is the family who has suffered by the father's continued and excessive absence.

You can't keep going 24/7. The lights won't always be green. If you don't slow down, sooner or later, you will come to a red light, and reluctantly will have to make a complete stop.

Moritz Erhardt, from Staufen, southwest Germany, was in the last few days of a seven-week internship at a U.S. bank's investment banking division in London when he was found dead at his lodgings on Aug. 15th 2013. His death highlighted concerns about interns working excessive hours and even through the night, after newspaper reports suggested that Erhardt had worked for 72 hours without sleep before he died.

All of us are aware of the need to rest. We know we need water, a healthy diet, and exercise. So often, our bodies give us a sign that it is time to rest, and the signals are loud and clear, but we completely ignore it, not realizing or caring about our limitations. If we would listen to what our bodies tell us, we would get enough rest. Unfortunately, we so often are caught up in the hustle and bustle of life and of earning more and more money that we don't listen to our own body. How many leaders—struck down by sickness—finally have been forced to rest, and for a long time too. Sooner or later, we will rest—one way or another.

Particularly, with the increasing demands leaders face and in these challenging times, the need for adequate rest is essential. It's a time to restore and renew. The word restoration means "the act of returning to an original state or condition." In adjective form, it means a "reinvigorating medicine" or "anything that reinvigorates."

The human body requires daily rest. Sleep plays an important role in your physical health. Sleep is involved in the healing and repair of your blood vessels and heart. Ongoing sleep deficiency is linked to an increased risk of heart disease, high blood pressure, kidney disease, diabetes, and stroke. Sleep helps your brain work properly. It also can affect how well you think, react, learn, work, and get along with others. Getting enough quality sleep at the right times helps you function well throughout the day. Physical fatigue makes us vulnerable to all kinds of temptations. I'm much more likely to get autocratic with people when I'm tired. Conflict is not far to follow. Exhaustion heightens negative emotions.Leaders who are sleep deficient are less productive. Studies also show that sleep deficiency alters activity in some parts of the brain. If you're sleep deficient, you may have trouble solving problems, making decisions, controlling your emotions and behaviour and coping with change. Your immune system relies on sleep to stay healthy. Ongoing sleep deficiency can also change the way in which your immune system responds. Sleep deprivation has also been linked to many traffic accidents, injuries, fatalities and even psychotic behaviour.

Sleep is more effective before than after midnight. Two hours of sleep before twelve o'clock is worth more than two hours after twelve o' clock. Therefore, if you went to bed at 9:00p.m., you would get six hours of quality rest by midnight. Try going to bed by 10:00p.m. to give the body a chance to repair its cells and bring healing wherever needed.

Traditionally, before the convenience of electricity, people would sleep during the hours of darkness and work in the light. In today's digital world, we have to guard against the inducement to work more than is healthy. Science discovered the circadian rhythms in which the body works on a daily 24-hour cycle, with specific release of hormones at certain times of the day. Studies performed in laboratories show a need for different kinds of sleep. Adult sleep requirements range from six to nine hours. People awake for 17 to 19 hours will perform at a level comparable to those who are intoxicated.

Some suggestions to help you have better sleep:

- ➲ Exercise daily

- ➲ Avoid tension and excitement before sleep

- ➲ Avoid eating for two to three hours before sleeping

- ➲ Avoid alcohol or caffeine

Sleep is nature's sweet restorer. It revitalizes and energizes the tired body. Rest is therefore basic, even fundamental to us as leaders, and by denying ourselves that needed rest, we are denying our basic humanity.While leadership is about execution, getting things done, and action, it also requires time to unplug, reflect, and renew. Your effectiveness and longevity as a leader depend directly on finding and establishing regular periods to recharge.

Alan Cohen stated, "There is virtue in work and there is virtue in rest. Use both and overlook neither."

YOUR ENVIRONMENT

A few years ago, a family of five went to a cabin in the mountains for a short Christmas vacation. One evening, they shut all the windows tight in order to keep cold air from coming in, and they turned the furnace on full blast in order to keep the cabin warm through the bitter night. The only problem, the whole family died because the furnace had used up all the oxygen in the air! As most of us know, we can live a few weeks without food, a few days without water, but only a few minutes without air.

Air is the most essential element needed to sustain life. Polluted air can lead to many serious and chronic disease conditions. With oxygen going to every organ of our body, we definitely need air as fresh and as clean as possible. Clean, fresh air is a vital component in maintaining good health. Air is a combination of gases in which oxygen forms about 21 percent of the total product. Our entire atmosphere weighs about five thousand trillion tons. Other component gases include nitrogen, argon, helium, hydrogen, and small amounts of trace gases.

Take a deep breath. Unless you have respiratory problems, it is so soothing.

Clean, fresh air is best suited to transfer oxygen to the blood through the lungs, and to carry off the carbon dioxide that the body produces. Fresh air is most present in natural environments where trees and flowing waters are found. Plants absorb the carbon dioxide in exchange for renewing the oxygen content of the air.

We should pursue all in our power to breathe the cleanest air possible. A person carries about two quarts of oxygen in the blood, lungs, and body tissues at any given time. Every cell in our bodies require air in order to function, and when that supply is severed, life cannot exist. Indeed, brain cells deprived of oxygen for more than four minutes begin to die, and the person will as well.

One of the great challenges that many people face, especially those living in cities or developed areas, is that the air often is dirty. In big cities, you need to find a nature park or garden with trees and plants to enjoy fresh air. Other factors working against fresh air include tobacco smoke, especially when it is circulated in confined spaces. Breathing polluted air can lead to numerous health problems including nausea, vomiting, migraine headaches, and eye and respiratory diseases.

In contrast, good, clean air usually may be found in abundance in natural outdoor environments, especially around green plants and near moving waters as lakes and rivers. Research has indicated that the algae in the ocean provides almost 90 percent of the oxygen in our atmosphere with the rest coming from plants. More oxygen also brings greater clarity to the brain. When you breathe fresh air, you can think better, as compared to when you remain inside an enclosed area for a longer period of time.

On my lunch hour, I usually go for a short walk in order to get some fresh air and sunlight. I literally take time to smell the buttercup flowers outside the office. I savour those moments. After just a few moments outside, a person often will feel refreshed and reinvigorated. Research shows that spending time in fresh air, surrounded by nature, increases energy in 90 percent of people. "Nature is fuel for the soul", states Richard Ryan, researcher and professor of psychology at the University of Rochester.

In just one year, the presence of trees saved 850 lives and prevented 670,000 cases of acute respiratory symptoms, according to new research published in the journal Environmental Pollution. Trees remove pollution from the air, making it healthier for us to take into our lungs.

Our individual situations vary; some people have a lifestyle in which all they breathe is fresh, clean air whilst others, due to where they live and work, might find fresh air a precious commodity that they yearn for as much as a poor person does financial security. If you are spending most of your time inside an air conditioned office or home, you will end up breathing in the same air over and over again. You are forcing your body to use stale air. By doing so, you are making it harder for your body to stay healthy.

In order to obtain optimal health, fresh air is vital. Whatever your situation, how important it is for you to take advantage of fresh air if you have access to it.

The word environment describes not only the physical atmosphere of air that surrounds us, but also, the attitudes, feelings, emotions of those around us, which creates an atmosphere that may be positive or negative. One may prosper or fail depending upon the nature of such atmospheres.

NATURE AS A SOURCE OF HEALTH

Nature supplies resources to satisfy our basic needs. Many people underestimate the benefits of spending time outdoors.

Science shows that you really should stop and smell the roses, as the smell of them promotes relaxation. Even walking through a park or your own backyard can improve your mood and help you feel calmer and happier when you catch a whiff of freshly cut grass.

"In every walk with nature one receives far more than he seeks." —John Muir

Nature also can be a source of healing to the body, mind, and soul. It can provide wellbeing. In many cases, being in nature can do wonders for us both physically and mentally. Doctors often will tell people to get away from the office and find rest and relaxation in a natural setting. Something in us resonates better with a field of flowers than it does with an asphalt parking lot.

SUNLIGHT

Sunlight is one of nature's most healing agents. It is essential; however, we do not need it every day.

On the body, there is a receptor site in most, if not *all cells* in the human body for Vitamin D. Regular exposure to sunlight enables your body to make adequate vitamin D. Getting adequate sunlight can reduce risks of some diseases. Sunlight helps to energize and strengthen your body, builds strong bone and teeth, kills germs in an out of the body, heals fungus infections, increases white blood cells, and builds your immune system. According to the World Health Organization, sun exposure has been used to successfully treat a number of diseases, including rickets, psoriasis, eczema and jaundice. Exposure to sunlight can also benefit those suffering from depression. It can improve your mood.

The strength of the sun's ultraviolet (UV) radiation is expressed as *UV Index*. It is primarily provided in daily weather *forecasts*. *UV index* identifies the strength of the ultraviolet (UV) radiation from the sun. It indicates the risk of overexposure on a scale from 0 (low) to 11 or more (extremely high). Therefore, the higher the index, the greater the risk of harm from unprotected sun exposure. UV radiation, has health benefits in moderation but in excess causes sunburn, skin aging, skin cancer, and eye damage. The effects of exposure to UV radiation accumulate over a lifetime. About 8 to 9 skin cancers in 10 are thought to be caused by excessive exposure to the sun.

According to the World Health Organization, getting anywhere from 5 to 15 minutes of casual sun exposure of hands, face and arms, two to three times a week during the summer months is sufficient to keep your vitamin D levels high.

Embrace the sunlight and Enjoy its life healing rays. It's free and good for you when handled wisely.

COPING WITH STRESS

Effective leaders know that stress can be a good thing. It keeps you focused and prompts action. If you're giving an important speech and you aren't; at least, a little anxious about it, you aren't going to do a good job. But, stress can also turn toxic.

When leaders are stressed, they usually don't treat themselves or others well.

Doctors report that between 75% percent and up to 90 percent of patients they see, come with stress-related complaints. Forty-three percent of all adults suffer adverse health effects from stress. Science has shown that when we are stressed, we release certain hormones that can affect various organs in our bodies. The human body is designed to experience stress and react to it. Stress can be positive "eustress", such as a getting a job promotion. It keeps us alert and ready to avoid danger. Stress becomes negative "distress" when a person faces continuous challenges without relief or relaxation between challenges. Stress, for example, can release adrenaline, which causes the heart to beat faster leading to palpitations. Some stress hormones cause the blood vessels to constrict, resulting in hypertension. Stress can also induce shallow and rapid breathing and in some cases even hyperventilation. If you have pre-existing respiratory problems like asthma or emphysema, stress can make it harder to breathe.

Stress can result in the diversion of blood from the stomach, causing digestive problems. Who has not felt what fear, anxiety, and worry can do to the stomach? Stress can cause an increase in blood glucose, which in some people can lead to diabetes. Stress hormones affect your respiratory and cardiovascular systems. Research suggests that stress also can bring on or worsen certain symptoms or diseases. Stress also is known to have a negative impact on our sleep, which in turn can have a negative impact on our overall health. Stress has been shown to affect negatively our immune system. The list can go on and on, so the point should be clear. We need to learn to effectively handle stress.

In 2014, after more than two years working as the CEO of Reddit, one of the most popular websites in the world, Yishan Wong resigned. He stated, "The job as CEO of Reddit is incredibly stressful and draining. After two and a half years, I'm basically completely worn out, and it was having significantly detrimental effects on my personal life. If anything, I probably pushed myself way too far—as a first-time CEO."

New scientific research have also identified the process by which chronic stress can actually cut our lifespan by shortening our telomeres (the "end caps" of our DNA strands), which play a big role in aging. The Occupational Safety and Health Administration (OSHA) declared stress a hazard of the workplace. Stress costs American industry more than $300 billion annually.

Researchers Thomas H. Holmes, and Richard H. Rahe developed the social readjustment rating scale, which lists life events with matching stress values for each: the death of spouse—100; personal injury or illness—53; change in residence—20; etc. A person accumulating 200 or more points at any given time runs a 50 percent chance of becoming ill; someone accruing 300 or more will reach a point of crisis. Moderate amounts of stress are necessary to increase performance, but beyond a point, stress becomes a health risk.

TAKING TIME FOR YOURSELF

Taking time for yourself is crucial to leadership. Take time to recharge. In top leadership positions, you tend to work a lot of long hours. Be careful not to overdo it. Even professional athletes know that pushing themselves at 100% all of the time does not yield gains in performance over the long term. Solitude and silence is one of the most important necessities of sustainable leadership. It's a time of rest, peace, strengthening, and refreshment. Distancing yourself from distractions and taking the time to listen to your thoughts is the path to wisdom.

"The best thinking has been done in solitude." —Thomas Edison

Your effectiveness and maybe even your longevity as a leader depend directly on finding and establishing regular periods of solitude.William Deresiewicz posits that our tech-saturated lives result in too much multitasking when we really need to spend time working through our questions and doubts, and formulating our own ideas away from the cacophony of voices that surround us."It is only through silence and stillness that we can come to our thoughts in any meaningful way and, from that spring, take action and we think best. Sadly, we have banished solitude. There is no time to think alone, intimately with who we are at our core." says Brian Tolle Partner of The Re-Wired Group.

Stillness allows for information to be absorbed and will give you a chance to focus. The competition may be steep and the market ever evolving, but effective leaders know they have to get it together and focus. Leaders that can appreciate the value of stillness can move forward and sustain momentum after pausing. Warren Buffet said, "I insist on a lot of time being spent, almost every day, to just sit and think. That is very uncommon in American business. I read and think,so I do more reading and thinking, and make less impulse decisions than most people in business."

"A wise woodcutter indeed is he who, rather than constantly chopping wood, will occasionally stop to sharpen his axe." — Unknown

Many individuals have a process to reflect daily. It may include activities like:

⮑ A daily walk alone with your thoughts

⮑ A routine time and place to stop and think, e.g.,a bench overlooking a special view, a long walk with your dog, etc.

⤳ Some spend time in prayer alone talking to God

⤳ Some even lie down and still their mind to reflect

SOCIAL SUPPORT

Being at the top can get lonely sometimes. As a leader, everyone is constantly looking to you for guidance, support, and direction. Leading can be stressful. There is no way to avoid the constant challenges of being responsible for people, outcomes, and uncertainties in the environment. It can be daunting at times when you don't have all the answers. Bottling up too much inside can be harmful. In difficult times, leaders often feel they need to keep information to themselves or make all the important calls alone. It doesn't matter how naturally talented you are, there are times you will need someone to lean on or open up to.

It is very clear that being isolated, lonely, and unloved increases the likelihood of various risky behaviours. Saddest of all, isolation deprives us of the joy of everyday life; the joy that comes from satisfying and fulfilling relationships. Success is not very fulfilling or joyous when there is no one to share it with. One study was conducted on 170 military wives receiving prenatal care at a military hospital. The research showed that women without emotional and psychological support had three times as many complications as those with adequate support. Anything that promotes a sense of isolation may lead to suffering and illness. That which promotes love and intimacy, connection, and community is healing and brings health. And no wonder, because as humans, we were meant to live in community and fellowship with one another.

"No man is an island entire of itself; every man is a piece of the continent, a part of the main."—John Donne.

All parts of the body interact to function effectively. If one part of the body suffers, all functions are affected. The closer we are to others, the more readily and powerfully we feel the impact of their problems. As a leader, you cannot achieve your goals alone. You need the support of your team and you need your own support system to get you through the tough times.

A doctor studied the importance of social ties and social support in relationship to disease and mortality rates. The close, social, cultural, and traditional ties of the Japanese culture made for exemplary health outcomes. The better the social ties, the better the health. He further indicated that social isolation results in poorer health and higher mortality rates. Meaningful social relationships positively influence physical, mental, and emotional behaviours.

Good relationships positively influence both our own and others' lives. Of course, there are times when we need to be alone, but that is not the same as being part of a larger community that can act as a support group, especially in times of need. As leaders, you need to surround yourself with the right friends and have a good support system. Sadly though, it may be difficult to trust or let others in after we have been burned by people only wanting to align with us for selfish motives. That's why it is important to have a tight knit inner circle that we can lean on in moments of distress; people who will encourage us and cheer us on to keep going, especially when the multitude is stoning us. Some days, you may not have the strength and may need a hand to get back up after you have been knocked down.

TRUST IN GOD

"Trust in the LORD with all thine heart; and lean not unto thine own understanding. In all thy ways, acknowledge Him, and He shall direct thy paths." —Proverbs 3:5-6

This promotes spiritual health. Numerous scientific publications have reported a connection between religious faith and positive mental and emotional well-being. Religious hope transcends the finite and focuses on the eternal. It's a hope found in the Creator, God, who alone can give us an assurance that this fleeting world can't.

Trusting in God provides an inner peace and stability. It gives strength in times of weakness, hope when all seems lost, and healing to unresolved problems. I spend my early mornings in prayer. Prayer allows one to talk to God, as you would to your best friend. Lay your plans before him and ask for direction. He is always there to comfort and guide. Maintain a daily connection with Him at least one hour out of your busy life and you will reap great rewards.

Always think positively and maintain a spirit of praise, as nothing tends more to promote health of body and of soul.

If we are going to enjoy a successful leadership journey. It's imperative we take care of ourselves physically and spiritually. Our physical and spiritual state affect our mental and emotional wellbeing. Only when we are healthy, can we perform at our optimum level to achieve the goals we set our sight on.

CHAPTER SIXTEEN

THE LEADER'S EMOTIONS

As humans, we are also emotional beings. One could argue justifiably that emotions rule our lives to a much greater extent than reason does or ever could. Emotions are a vital part of the human personality. They can be powerful motivators, both for good and for bad. And, depending on the emotions, they make us happy, sad, fearful, or joyous. Leaders need to have high Emotional Intelligence (EI) to manage the emotions of themselves and others in order to be successful. Good leadership begins with EI. EI accounts for 85 to 90 percent of the difference between outstanding and average leaders. Emotions play a bigger part than people think. They affect culture and climate, which affects business performance. People "feed" off each other's emotions.

Every emotion stimulates a chemical response in your body. Positive emotions cause the production of the "feel good" hormones serotonin and dopamine. Negative emotions cause the production of the "stress" hormones cortisol and adrenaline. Positive emotions can bring a feeling of fulfilment and wellbeing; negative ones tend to cause pain and torment. Positive emotions can promote mental health whilst a prolonged exposure to negative emotions may bring about behavioural and interpersonal problems. It is impossible to avoid negative emotions altogether because to live is to experience disappointment and conflicts. Negative emotions stop us from thinking and behaving rationally and seeing situations in their true perspective. They can dampen our enthusiasm for life depending on how long we let them affect us and the way we choose to express them. Thus, emotions play a significant part in our overall wellbeing.

Negative emotional states, such as worry, fear, anger, and jealousy produce immediate physiological responses: increased heart rate, tense muscles, dryness of the mouth, and other physical manifestations. Research shows that even one five-minute episode of anger is so stressful that it can impair your immune system for more than six hours. Poorly managed anger is also related to a slew of health conditions, such as hypertension, cardiovascular disease, digestive disorders, and infection. All of these health issues can lead to more serious problems, such as heart attacks and stroke.

In contrast, positive emotional states, such as compassion, kindness, and gratitude are associated with a sense of well-being and a positive outlook. Positive psychology aims at the promotion of positive emotions in order to obtain happiness and to prevent mental illness. Emotional distress can weaken your body's immune system, making you more likely to get colds and other infections during emotionally difficult times. Negativity—from yourself, circumstances, or others in your life—has been scientifically proven to be the emotional root of many diseases. Harbouring certain negative emotions will adversely affect health and longevity; in contrast, the promotion of a positive outlook can promote health and longevity. In other words, the more positive your outlook and emotions, the better overall health you can enjoy.

Health professionals today recognize the close link between psychological stress and physical maladies. The expression "psychosomatic disease" has been part of the health professionals' vocabulary for years, and it refers to physical symptoms caused largely by psychological processes. There is such a close relationship between the mind and the body, when one becomes ill, the other does, too. In recent times, the field of psychoneuroimmunology has identified the key role that mental states play in protecting our bodies from diseases. Did you know that more than fifty percent of all illnesses we suffer are of mental origin?

In the following section, we will look at some of the negative emotions leaders face and how we can effectively deal with them.

FEAR

Fear about what *may* happen, is one of the most dangerous emotions for mental and physical health. A medieval legend tells of the traveller who one night met Fear and Plague on their way to London where they expected to kill 10,000 people. The traveller asked Plague if he would do all the killing. "Oh no," Plague answered. "I shall kill only a few hundred. My friend **Fear** will kill the rest."

Years ago, television viewers were subjected to a show called Fear Factor, in which contestants were placed in various fearful situations: from sitting in a pit filled with scorpions to walking through a building that was on fire—all in order to see how they would deal with fear. Of course, one doesn't need to construct fear. Life itself is full of things that cause us to be fearful. A seventeenth century British political philosopher, Thomas Hobbes, wrote that fear was the prime and motivating factor in all human life. No matter who you are and where you live, fear is an ever-present part of our lives. Fear though, in and of itself, isn't always bad. Fear is a natural and necessary emotion that helps humans cope with danger and helps them survive.

Leaders may face fear when assuming a new role, undertaking new projects or at the outcome of a failed project. Fear is a very stressful emotion; one that can take a powerful physical toll on our bodies. Fear is not merely limited to what it does to our minds; it can have a very harmful effect on our bodies. The only way to *deal with fear* is to face it. Begin by determining exactly what you're afraid of. Ask questions like, "What is it about this that scares me?" Be aware of your self-talk. "What are you constantly saying to yourself?" Your subconscious is listening. Lastly, always visualize positive results.

SELF ESTEEM AND CONFIDENCE

One of the great struggles that many people face is the sense of their own self-worth. What are we worth in this world? What can one life mean amid teeming billions? We sense massive forces over which we have no control. A nineteenth century thinker, Arthur Schopenhauer, while deep in thought about the essence of human identity, accidently bumped into someone on the street. The person whom he hit angrily demanded, "Who do you think you are?" "Who am I?" Schopenhauer responded. "I wish I knew."

Low self-esteem is a modern epidemic. In everyday existence, low self-esteem never may reach clinical extent, but it almost always affects relationships and impairs performance in most areas of our life. One of the main reasons people suffer more than ever from this problem is the media, which often portrays its celebrities and successful leaders as larger than life, leaving others to feel their own inadequacy. Successful people mainly highlight their successes and hardly mention their struggles or failures.

Self-esteem is your inner voice which tells you whether you are good enough to do or achieve something. Self-esteem is about how we value ourselves; our perceptions and beliefs in who we are and what we are capable of doing. Our concept of self is often shaped by the reaction others display, based on their outward observation of us. If everyone tells you that you are smart, you will be more likely to view yourself as smart. Self-perceptions: what I see in myself is one important component of self-esteem. There is a great deal of error when one judges oneself in terms of looks, and ability, etc. There always are going to be people better looking and more talented than you. Individuals experiencing poor self-esteem need to think in terms of personal attributes that are of great value and not necessarily what the superficial world values. Most societies tend to place excessive value in outward, observable features. However, other traits, such as honesty, kindness, temperance, and humility tend to have less value.

There is a desirable middle area between extremely low self-esteem and arrogance. Too much confidence can make you come off as cocky and cause you to stumble into unforeseen obstacles.

This leadership journey requires confidence in yourself and in your abilities; otherwise, you will be beaten down and trampled by the dissenters and naysayers. You can't take over the world with a low esteem of yourself. Your level of self-confidence can show in many ways; your behaviour, your body language, how you speak, and what you say. It all comes down to one simple question: If you don't believe in yourself, how do you expect anybody else to? Taking risks and seizing opportunities requires you to believe in your ability to succeed.

Subsequently, as a leader, the influence that you have on others' self-esteem is extremely powerful. More than you realize, you have the ability to shape others' self-concepts through words, actions, and even how we look at them.

WORRY AND ANXIETY

Worrying is being overly concerned about a situation or problem. With excessive worrying, your mind and body go into overdrive, as you repetitively focus on "what might happen." Worry is useless and futile. Evaluating problems in order to find possible solutions may be productive, but worrying does nothing to solve the issue, but expands the negative side of things. Excessive worrying may lead to anxiety. Anxiety is a feeling of worry, nervousness, or unease about something with an uncertain outcome. It is manifested through distress about uncertainties. Such uncertainties may not even happen; as they occur only in the mind. Yet, the symptoms of anxiety are quite real, both emotionally and physically, and can be agonising.

In 2011, Aaron's, Inc. president and chief executive officer, Robin C. Loudermilk, Jr., abruptly stepped down from his position. He cited anxiety as the reason for his exit. "Robin has struggled with anxiety and other similar issues for years," said Gilbert Danielson, executive vice president and chief financial officer of the rent-to-own furniture company. "With increasing demands and stress of being CEO of a large and growing public company, he feels he would now rather invest his future time and attention on his health."

In some counselling sessions, clients act out roles relevant to situations in order to better handle them. In addition, they learn how to manage their thoughts when faced with anxiety. They also are taught relaxation and breathing techniques to be used in critical situations.

Winston Churchill said: "I remember the story of the old man who said on his deathbed that he had a lot of trouble in his life; most of which had never happened."

The following list shows the various things that make up an average person's anxiety. Anxious individuals focus on:

- ⮑ 50% of events that will never happen

- ⮑ 25% of occurrences that cannot be changed

- ⮑ 10% about unconfirmed criticism by others

- ⮑ 10% about health

- ⮑ 5% about real problems that will be faced

Life is all about perspective. Clean your spectacles in which you view the world and life. Messages and experiences from the past have a way of changing the filter through which we look at the rest of the world. Not everything will go as planned and that is okay, but the more we try to control things, the more we tend to worry. The more you are able to look your uncertainty in the face and tolerate it, the less power it will have over you.

Contentment is an effective antidote for worry. Contentment is not an inheritable attitude, but an acquired characteristic. Contentment as a mental or emotional state of satisfaction maybe drawn from being at ease in one's situation, body, and mind. It is a crucial component of happiness and psychological wellbeing. Being content means to work on the present, but also, acceptance of the past and looking at the future with hope. Having everything doesn't guarantee contentment and happiness. For some people, no matter what they have, it's never enough. Others, having so little, are nevertheless satisfied.

One of the many current definitions of "intelligence", alike to contentment, is the ability to adapt to new situations. The pursuit of contentment is a central theme in many philosophical and religious schools across diverse cultures.

In today's world, we face so many problems. There is a need to develop a sense of contentment for what we presently have and not to worry about what might come tomorrow.

"If your emotional abilities aren't in hand, if you don't have self-awareness, if you are not able to manage your distressing emotions, if you can't have empathy and have effective relationships, then no matter how smart you are, you are not going to get very far."—Daniel Goleman

ANGER, HATE AND JEALOUSY

If you truly want be successful in your leadership journey, you have to travel lightly.

We can distinguish between anger and hatred in two ways: intensity and duration. Anger might be triggered when someone does something that frustrates us. It tends to come and go. On the other hand, hatred lasts longer and is more pervasive. It tends to overwhelm us and obscure everything else we might feel. It makes us want to take action; to hurt or destroy whatever inspires the hatred.

It's difficult to improve your life if you are filled with hostility or consumed by deep-rooted hate. We all get angry from time to time. Anger is a common human emotion. If you don't let go of the hatred, it will continue to grow and to eat away at your life. Like all negative emotions, if left unchecked, your anger could ultimately destroy your life. If you're in this type of a situation where you are extremely angry, try to put things in perspective. Is your anger or hatred going to accomplish anything positive or in any way, going to improve your life or anybody else's?

Anger is a powerful emotion. When it gets out of control, it can turn destructive. It impairs your judgment, has a negative impact on the way people see you (destroys relationships), and often gets in the way of success.

"A patient man has great understanding, but a quick-tempered man displays folly" —Proverbs 14:29

AOL's CEO, Tim Armstrong's inordinate and uncontrolled anger resulted in the impulsive firing of an employee for taking his picture. This took place at a company meeting and was done in front of a thousand employees. He was later forced to make a public apology. However, by then, the damage had already been done because he had lost the respect of most of his team.

One of my employees hated another teammate because he underhandedly took a promotion from him by befriending him. At first, it was unnoticeable but then his emotions became irrepressible. It got so out of control, he would end up arguing in meetings with his colleague. He became intensely jealous of him. Even if this colleague had a good proposal, he would never support it. He would always find ways that it wouldn't work, all because of his personal feelings. For anyone that supported the colleague, he got upset with them because they weren't taking his side. It became like a conspiracy to him and unbearable to his peers. Another destructive emotion is jealousy. **Jealousy** tends to be personal; it targets an individual who is perceived as a rival and a threat. As a result, jealousy often causes violence; either psychological (verbal abuse, backbiting, criticism) or physical. I urgently recommended that this employee take some time off to deal with what happened and how it affected him, so he could move forward and if required, get expert help either from a professional or his religious leader because this was destroying him.

GUILT AND SHAME

Guilt and shame sometimes go hand in hand; the same action may give rise to feelings of both shame and guilt where the former reflects how we feel about *ourselves* and the latter involves an awareness that our actions have injured *someone else*. In other words, shame relates to self, and guilt to others.

Shame is the painful feeling arising from the consciousness of something dishonourable, improper, and ridiculous, etc., done by oneself or another. We don't want others to be aware of our failures; this can make us feel embarrassed. Additionally, I can't tell you the numerous times early in my career that I was overcome with shame due to mistakes in pronunciation of a word in an important presentation. As a leader, you want to be taken seriously; you don't want to be a laughingstock.

A leader may suffer guilt due to failure, letting people down, or making a poor decision. You are only human; you will make mistakes. A sense of guilt is one of the most painful and incapacitating emotional experiences. Sometimes; however, the guilt mechanism makes people feel guilty about something for which they are not responsible, as in the case of some accident survivors or children of divorce. But, when the sense of guilt is justified, it serves as a good conscience. Guilt produces enough discomfort to make the person do something about it. Depending on personal choices, guilt may be highly destructive.

People affected by guilt think on it repeatedly; feeling bad for what they did, wishing they could have done differently, and entering into self-blame. Such meditation produces much distress, frustration, and anger at oneself for not having done differently. Unfortunately, no matter how much time is focused on recalling the past, it can't be changed. The truth is, since we only live in the present, we can only change the present. Consequently, our current actions and present way of life will definitely affect our life tomorrow. Since we can't change what we did yesterday, we can change what we do tomorrow; therefore, we shouldn't waste time today dwelling on the past. Truthful confession is good for the soul, and seemingly, also for the body. Repentance and forgiveness are required… forgiving others and at times yourself.

Psychologists generally define **forgiveness** as a conscious, deliberate decision to release feelings of resentment or vengeance toward a person or group who has harmed you regardless of whether they actually deserve your forgiveness. In certain contexts, forgiveness is a legal term for absolving or giving up all claims on account of debt, loan, obligation, or other claims.

Forgiveness does not mean forgetting nor does it mean condoning or excusing offenses. Instead, forgiveness brings the forgiver peace of mind and frees him or her from corrosive anger.

The Stanford Forgiveness Project trained 260 adults in forgiveness in a six-week course:

- ⊃ 70% reported a decrease in their feelings of hurt

- ⊃ 13% experienced reduced anger

- ⊃ 27% experienced fewer physical complaints (for example, pain, gastrointestinal upset, dizziness, etc.)

The practice of forgiveness has also been linked to better immune function and a longer lifespan. Other studies have shown that forgiveness has more than just a figurative effect on the heart; it can actually lower our blood pressure and improve cardiovascular health as well.

An attitude of **Gratitude** always wins. Acknowledging the positive aspects of life and giving thanks has a powerful impact on emotional wellbeing. It is important to have an attitude of gratitude so you will constantly be aware of the blessings in your life. You will be magnifying the positives and not the negatives. When we are grateful we leave the door open for more blessings to come our way. Dr. Emmons and Dr. McCullough did extensive research into the effects of gratitude practices. In one study in 2003, they found that after 10 weeks, the people who had focused on gratitude for their lives showed significantly more *optimism* in many areas of their lives including health and exercise.

DEPRESSION AND DESPAIR

Depression is a common affliction today. Along with the general sadness that accompanies depression, there is the loss of enjoyment of those things that formerly were pleasurable. Sufferers experience tiredness, a sense of hopelessness, and a loss of energy, sleeping either not enough or too much, feelings of low self-esteem, and/or thoughts of death and suicide. Various physical symptoms, such as digestive problems, headaches, and backache, among others often result. Some people experience just one or two symptoms while others manifest several and suffer for months until the episode ends. In any case, the burden of depression is enormous and must be relieved by medical and spiritual intervention. If not recognized and treated, in most cases, severe depression may lead to suicide.

This is a problem in all age groups, but in some societies, those 25 years and younger are particularly vulnerable. There are two main kinds of depression. The first occurs in response to disagreeable situations in life. The other kind of depression is related to chemical imbalances in the central nervous system. The latter is genetic and is a disease which needs medical intervention. It's important for leaders to recognize these symptoms in themselves and others.

In recent times, I had to refer an employee for counselling who wanted to commit suicide. Her parents had divorced and she wasn't getting along with her father. He had become verbally abusive to her. Her mother was diagnosed with a terminal illness. On top of that, her boyfriend was unfaithful. She felt it was too much to handle. Today though, she is doing quite well.

Hopelessness is a symptom of depression, and the message of hope can offer so much in contrast to a world that offers so little. Of course, when depression is severe, it's important to get professional help. When one sees oneself negatively "I am stupid", looks at the world pessimistically "I hate my life", and contemplates the future hopelessly "it will only get worse", chances of depression become high. This attitude is called "catastrophic thinking".

It all boils down to how you look at:

➲ Yourself

⊃ The world

⊃ The future

We should always be hopeful and look with the eyes of optimism and positivity.

RESILIENCE

Resilience is the process of facing adversity and "bouncing back" successfully without becoming negatively affected by the experience. It is the ability to keep pressing on even in the midst of adverse circumstances. Dr. Andrew Weil describes resilience as being like a rubber band—no matter how far a resilient person is stretched or pulled by negative emotions, he or she has the ability to bounce back to his or her original state. The concept has received growing attention because of the advantage of possessing an adequate amount of resilience in the face of life's difficulties. Leaders need thick skin. For American poet, Robert Frost, the woods were "lovely, dark, and deep. . . but I have promises to keep and miles to go before I sleep."

"Life doesn't get easier or more forgiving; we get stronger and more resilient." —Steve Maraboli

People with resilience are better able to cope with stress in a healthy way. Resilience can be developed with different strategies. These include having social support and keeping a positive outlook. Others may need the help of a therapist to achieve this goal with cognitive behavioural therapy (CBT).

241

POSITIVE THINKING

As one of the most utilized forms of mental health intervention today, cognitive behavioural therapy (CBT) is based on the assumption that most psychological problems are improved by identifying and changing inaccurate and dysfunctional perceptions, thoughts, and behaviours. CBT is one of the most popular forms of therapy in the field of Psychology (Beck & Beck, 2011). People with depression tend to interpret facts negatively, people with anxiety tend to look at the future with apprehension, and those with low self-esteem maximize others' success and minimize their own. The goal of CBT is to see beyond the diagnosis and to look at the person as a whole to decide what needs to be "fixed" (Kaplan & Saccuzzo, 2013). CBT; therefore, trains people to identify and change their unhealthy thinking habits into better alternatives that promote desirable behaviour and eliminate unwanted ones.

Words are very powerful tools, either for good or for evil. Thoughts and words have power. Our words either build up or tear down. There is life and death in the power of the tongue. It's just as important to remember: **we also adversely can affect others' thinking by expressing our negativity to others.** How careful must we then be with the words that we speak to others and ourselves?

It's very important to build others up. When you build others up, you are actually building up yourself. Ponder for a moment how good you feel when you reach out and help others. There is a sense of wellbeing; we get a satisfaction that nothing else can match, by giving of ourselves. A Chinese farmer was tending his rice paddy up in the mountain terraces overlooking the sea. One day, he saw the beginning of a tidal wave—the sea had retreated, leaving a wide portion of the bay exposed, and he knew that the water would return with strength, extinguishing everything in the valley. He thought of his friends working in the valley and decided to set his rice field on fire. His friends instantly ran up the mountain to put the fire out; thus, missing being killed in the tidal wave. As a result of this spirit of helping one another, their lives were saved. No wonder scientific studies confirm that positive medical benefits can occur from doing good for others. It makes perfect sense: by helpings others, we feel better, and when we feel better, our physical being is improved.

Healthy, positive thinking and speaking empowers us. It lifts us up while also strengthening us to overcome challenges. No good leader ever reaches the end of their leadership journey and thinks, "I wish I'd been a crueller person. I wish I'd hated more and been jealous more often." You have the ability to add years to your life by channelling your thoughts in a positive way.

Negative emotions exist for a purpose. They protect us and make us aware of dangers. Negative emotions prompt us to act upon our current circumstance and generate positive changes, such as anger (Biswar-Diener & Kashdan, 2014).Fear helps you react to danger, anxiety makes you more aware of potential threats around you, and guilt makes you reconsider past actions that may have been harmful to others, and make amends with them (Rosen, 2008; Tibbetts, 2003).But, prolonged exposure to negative emotions can be detrimental to our emotional and physical health.

As we all know in life, you are either solving a problem, coming out of a problem, or heading into a new problem. If we get in the habit of not allowing negative thoughts and ideas to saturate our mind, we will have greater peace of mind and emotional well-being. The better able you are in managing negative emotions, the smoother the road will be.

HOW TO DEAL WITH NEGATIVE EMOTIONS:

- ⟳ *Take some time to analyze what your predominant feelings are.* As one doctor told his patient; "Tell me what feelings you harbour in your soul, and I'll tell you what your health will be like."

- ⟳ *Acknowledge your feelings.* If you can admit how you are feeling, then you can begin to tackle those emotions and find a solution to the problem.

- *Don't blow things out of proportion* by replaying them over and over in your mind. Constantly going over negative events robs you from enjoying the present and makes you feel miserable.

- *Let go of the past* and unhealthy thought patterns. Take things one day at a time. Accept certain situations and move on. Think positive thoughts. If you find yourself always thinking the worst about others and/or yourself, try to retrain your mind to think more positively. *Don't take things personally.*

- *Know yourself and your response.* Be aware how negative emotions make you feel and which events trigger those feelings, so you can prepare in advance. Replace negative thoughts with positive thoughts.

  "Promise yourself to be so strong that nothing can disturb your peace of mind. Look at the sunny side of everything and make your optimism come true." — *Christian D. Larson*

- *Have a close inner circle you can confide in.* Sometimes, just talking to a close friend, family member, or even a therapist about something that is bothering you can help to alleviate the negative feelings you are having. Talk about it, and then move on. If you keep speaking about it, it can be likened to picking the scab off a wound. It will keep bleeding afresh and never heal.

- *Remove yourself from the situation.* Let your emotions subside. You don't want to say or do something you may later regret. Take a break, go for a walk, or take deep breaths until you have calmed down. Allow yourself to relax. Once your mind is calm, you can and will be able to control your emotions in a more efficient manner.

As we have seen, a positive outlook has numerous benefits. As leaders we have so many responsibilities and deal with mounting challenges coupled with conflicting personalities. We without a doubt, need a healthy emotional state to make good decisions and to build and retain trust with our team. How much care and mental discipline should we practice then, in order to prevent disturbance in our emotions which can cloud our judgement. Our body reacts better when we feel positive, happy, and content. Today, choose the positive path and allow positive emotions as love, joy, and peace to infuse your life and those who come into contact with you. Be inspired and inspire others. Uplift others and be at peace with the person you are and the path you are taking. Live your best life now! Lead with Emotional Intelligence!

CHAPTER SEVENTEEN

TIME MANAGEMENT:
A Key to a Leader's Effectiveness

Do you wish there were more hours in a day? Does it seem like you have more tasks than time?

Leaders today are swamped with phone calls, conversations, back-to-back meetings, emails and it's all happening at the same time. The issue is not whether we have enough time. The real issue is *how we choose to spend the time we have.* We all have the same 24 hours every day, yet some leaders are more efficient with their time. The big challenge for attention is sorting out what's urgent from what's just an interruption. Every time you focus on a distraction, you have lost time that could have been spent getting urgent things done. To achieve overall success, a leader needs to have effective time management skills. Time management is about managing ourselves in relation to time.

We are in the age of information overload. People on average take in five times more information today than they did 20 years ago. And, it takes considerable time to digest all this information. Teresa Amabile and Steven Kramer, psychologists at Harvard Business School, studied 238 members of teams engaged in projects, from designing new kitchen equipment to multifaceted information technology systems. The team members kept diaries of their work days including how productive they found each day. The most productive and satisfying days, came when they were able to have uninterrupted time to focus on their project.

"Until we can manage time, we can manage nothing else."
—PeterDrucker

HOW TO MANAGE YOUR TIME WITH 10 TIPS THAT WORK:

➲ **Set Up Your Workspace.** A cluttered workspace covered with documents can affect a leader's productivity. Time can be wasted if your work area is not organized well. Your desk should be clear of all paper except the specific job on hand. Don't let paperwork pile up.

➲ **Plan Your Day. Write everything down.** Take the first 30 minutes of every day to plan your day. Don't start your day until you complete your time plan. Creating to-do lists can help you keep track of daily tasks you need to complete, and help you plan your time accordingly. Start each day the night before, mentally listing the priorities for the following day. During the day, pay attention to what's stopping you from reaching your goals and what needs to be done to move forward. Highly successful leaders monitor the results they achieve with their time. By keeping track of how they spend their time, they determine when they're off course and take steps to get back on track.

- ⮡ **Organize and Prioritize.** Prioritize tasks and make lists. Start with the most urgent, and work your way down the list. See that your time is spent as per your priorities or your core responsibilities. Being organized helps you to be on top of everything. Multi-tasking might seem like a good skill, but it actually makes all your work suffer. Instead, prioritize each task every day and focus on one at a time. Instead of spreading yourself thin by concentrating on several goals at once, invest your mental focus on one goal; the most important one. You'll get better quality plus the sense of satisfaction as you check off each item.

The Urgent/Important Matrix: This concept is called the Eisenhower Principle. It is said to be how former US President Dwight Eisenhower organized his tasks. When you are prioritizing, choose a goal that will have the greatest impact on your life compared to how long it will take to achieve.

Tasks can generally be placed into one of four groups:

- ⮡ Urgent and important

- ⮡ Important, but not urgent

- ⮡ Urgent, but not important

- ⮡ Not urgent and not important

IMPORTANT: These are activities that lead to achieving your goals and have the greatest impact on your life.

URGENT: These activities demand immediate attention, but are often associated with someone else's goals rather than our own.

⮑ **Delegate Well.** Are you finding your to-do lists getting longer and longer? Stop procrastinating. Instead of being overwhelmed by a large project, break it down into a smaller, bite-sized tasks. You don't need to be responsible for the menial tasks. Everything does not have to go through you. Calculate what your time is worth. Productive leaders know that if their time is worth $200 an hour, they shouldn't be spending time doing minimum wage jobs. Leaders see delegation as proper arrangement of resources, such as the best people for the job are matched with the right opportunities. Proper delegation can save leaders time and help them to focus on areas where they're most skilled.

⮑ **Take control of your Schedule**. It's important to master the art of scheduling appointments efficiently in order to maximize productivity. Biting off more than you can chew is one of the leading ways to complicate things. Know your limit and stay within it. Productive leaders *plan for interruptions* and schedule time into their calendar—for urgent meetings, calls, and emergencies during the day. Leave empty blocks of time in your schedule. Block off quiet time to work at your desk without interruptions—no phone calls, meetings, or visitors dropping in unannounced. Make sure that people know you're unavailable from 10 a.m. to 11 a.m. or whenever you find yourself working most productively.

⊃ **Limit Email consumption and production**. Don't underestimate the power of "Yes"or "No".Looking back, I would spend considerable time drafting lengthy responses to emails that I could have just answered with a"Yes" or "No". You just have to diligent in deciphering which cases these short responses would be applicable to. If you're spending critical time doing tasks that are not related to your core priorities, you can end up wasting a whole day, and you haven't accomplished anything because you've spent the entire day sending or responding to emails.

⊃ **Set and stick to deadlines. Stay Focused** on Your Goals and Priorities. Your ability to focus attention on a task is crucial for achieving goals. It's no surprise that attention spans have been decreasing over the past decade due to technology and information overload. According to *statisticbrain.com*, the average attention span of a healthy adult today is just 20 minutes. If you want to get things done, you need to stick to and set a realistic timeframe. Schedule everything, put goals in writing, and hold yourself accountable.

⊃ **Monitor Time You Spend Online.** Spending time on your computer and phone can present distractions for leaders. Every minute a notification or message alert pops up. Monitor how you spend your time online to determine whether you're focusing on the tasks that matter most to your business. Productive leaders do not let technology control them. Block out distractions as LinkedIn and other forms of social media unless you use these tools for business. Individuals who let technology control them, as opposed to them controlling the technology have become addicts. Technology should be an asset, not a distraction.

In 2013, Former Swisscom CEO, Carsten Schloter, committed suicide amid indications that the head of Switzerland's telecoms giant suffered from permanent stress and had become dangerously addicted to his smartphone since the breakup of his marriage in 2009. "Modern communications devices have their downside," Schloter told Switzerland's Schweiz am Sonntag in May, "The most dangerous thing is to fall into a mode of permanent activity and continuously consult one's smartphone to see whether any new mails have come in. Everyone should switch off their mobile phone from time to time." Referring to the lack of "windows" in which he could be free of work and family responsibilities, he said: "It makes you feel as if you are being strangled. I always have the feeling that there should be less responsibilities."

- ⮑ **Encourage a solutions-focused** and not a problem-focused culture. Do not let your subordinates come to you with problems unless they bring their proposed solutions. This is a very effective time saver. It will cause them to think or delay, bombarding you with things they could fix themselves.

- ⮑ Don't take your work home. Even if you work from home, don't be on call the entire day. I have one day for a week which is my rest day. On Saturday's I stop and recharge. If you do have to bring work home, don't make it a habit. This will take away valuable time you should be spending with your family. Have hours in the evening that you are away from your phone. Eat dinner with your family every night. Studies show that families that eat dinner together are closer. You do not need to check and respond to every email instantly. The world will not end and the company will not fall apart.

In most organizations I have consulted with, I have noticed that meetings are one the greatest culprits of time wasters.

Tips to make meetings more effective:

➲ Try to say 'No' to a meeting where you are not required.

➲ Suggest start and finish times for meetings and strictly adhere to them. (Remember, after 45 minutes, most meetings lose steam.) When possible, use conference calls and web conferences to save time.

➲ Agenda should be definite. Everyone should receive the agenda and relevant documents well in advance.

⮑ Encourage everyone to come prepared (with facts and figures). Request they talk to the point (keep it short and simple), and do not try to divert the discussion.

⮑ There should be a set finishing time for meetings.

⮑ Be strict with deadlines, but be flexible enough to accommodate individual situations.

Make the Telephone work for you:

⮑ Plan your calls.

⮑ Set aside a period of time for making and receiving calls (if possible).

⮑ If someone calls, let them know you are in the middle of something, "but how may I help you." This will let them know to get to the point quickly.

When you're interrupted, practice asking yourself: Can this wait? Leaders need to decide what matters now, and then make that relay this with a strong sense of goodwill. **Communicate your availability.** Does your team know whether it's okay to interrupt you? Kindly, let them know that you are in the middle of something and will get to their task, when you are finished. Identify your time wasters and resolve to eliminate them. Leaders need to be strong about the boundaries of their attention. Do not become entangled by the wealth of information around you; get the urgent things done, and only pay attention to what's relevant to that.

The 80/20 rule, also known as Pareto's Principle, states that 80% of your results come from only 20% of your actions. It definitely comes down to analyzing what you are spending your time on. Are you focusing in on the 20% of activities that produce 80% of the results? Every day, when you come to the office, look at your schedule and ask yourself where to start? It must be 20% if you want effective results. Additionally know your mental peak that's the time in the day where you perform at an optimum level. This is what people call your personal Einstein Window.

Don't let work fill up your entire evening and break other arrangements. **Parkinson's Law** is the adage that "work expands so as to fill the time available for its completion", so the more time you make available, the more your day will go by. Successful people end their working day at a fixed time. There must be a cut off time.

A hectic schedule may make us lose sight of the truly important things. Daily routines may distract us from what we believe to be fundamental. Having a stringent schedule is great, but never forget that your most important resource is people. Many leaders have strict routines so much that they don't make time for people.

I always remembered this story my pastor told that had left him with deep guilt at that point in time. One Saturday evening, he was on his way to a board meeting, which he was already late for. A stranger came to his house wanting to speak with him. He told him kindly he was quite busy, but asked for his address and phone number so he could visit him on his return. When the meeting finished about two hours later, he went to the given address, but there was a large tent and a gathering of people. Upon inquiring he learned the man had committed suicide. His mother had sent the man to visit the pastor as a last resort since he was very depressed and threatened to kill himself.

Effective time management employs a careful balance between stringent schedules and making time to establish deep connections with people. The best leaders are able to successfully master this skill. They get things done and they make time for people. Time is our most precious commodity because it is limited. We can generate more wealth, but we cannot produce more time. When we give someone our time, we really give a portion of our life that we can never get back. Our time is our life.

Successful leaders take a holistic approach to managing their time, as they realize the importance of maintaining a healthy mind, body, spirit, and emotional state.

CHAPTER EIGHTEEN

The Ultimate Leader: 26 Traits—A to Z of Leadership

Leadership is a mysterious and dynamic complexity that is a never ending journey of discovery (Schaeffer, 2002). There is a blending of character traits and techniques that gives a leader the required formula to reach a desired goal. *To err is human; however, and the strongest and most influential leaders today*

have undergone significant transformation during their lifetime (Satell, 2014). Successful leadership demands certain skills and qualities in the leader.

HERE ARE 26 ESSENTIAL QUALITIES THAT PAINT A PORTRAIT OF "THE ULTIMATE LEADER"

A for Authentic: Authentic leadership is an approach to leadership that emphasizes building the leader's legitimacy through honest relationships with followers, and is built on an ethical foundation. Generally, authentic leaders are positive people with truthful self-concepts who promote openness. If leadership is not authentic, then what is it? Authenticity acts as a catalyst that earns the respect of followers. Authenticity is critical when directing others since it builds trust, and followers love leaders they can trust. By building trust and generating enthusiastic support from their subordinates, authentic leaders are able to improve an individual and team performance. The more your team trusts you, the easier they will follow your lead.

In order to be an effective and influential leader today, one must begin by making an honest and authentic assessment of oneself (Kruse, 2013).

B for Brave: A leader must be courageous and decisive. *This will manifest itself by confronting challenges head-on, seeking feedback, saying what needs to be said, and holding others and oneself accountable for results* (Tardanico, 2013). Aristotle called courage the first virtue because it makes all of the other virtues possible. Leadership takes courage. Followers want leaders who make decisions conclusively, who interpret situations with rational and emotional intelligence, and who exude confidence. Leadership takes making bold and often unpopular decisions. Bravery is not being devoid of fear; rather, it is an act of courage in the face of fear. The leader who recognizes fear, and then faces this fear courageously has demonstrated bravery.

C for Communication Skills: *Seventy percent of an individual's time is spent communicating. Typically, forty five percent of this time is spent listening and thirty percent speaking* (Adler, Rosenfeld, Proctor, 2001). "If a leader can't get a message across clearly and motivate others to act on it, then having a message doesn't even matter." —Gilbert Amelio. Leadership is about influencing. Good communication skills are essential for effective leadership. Great leaders are passionate and enthusiastic about their vision and this creates a ripple effect in the organization. Knowing what needs to be done is one thing, but communicating that and inspiring others to jump on that boat is another thing. Always keep your team informed. Be open and honest. Listen with the intention of understanding. Great leaders understand the art of communication to effectively get their message across. First, you must realize and accept that clear communication is a two-way process. It's not enough to speak clearly; you have to make sure you're being understood and accept feedback.

Here are six tips for effective Communication:

1 **Prepare how you'll communicate.** Clarify the goal of the communication. What do you really want to convey?

2 **Decide the communication channel** whether email, meeting, or face to face interaction. Plan carefully and anticipate the receiver's viewpoint and feelings.

3 **Deliver the message.** Confirm if the recipient understands.

4 **Receive feedback.** Keep an open mind.

5 **Evaluate the effectiveness of the communication afterward.** Were there any barriers to getting your message across clearly?

6 **Take corrective action as necessary.**

"If you want to build a ship, don't drum up the men to gather wood, divide the work, and give orders. Instead, teach them

to yearn for the vast and endless sea" —Antoine de Saint Exupéry

D for Determination: Determination is the desire to get the job done and includes characteristics such as initiative, persistence, dominance, and drive. People with determination are willing to assert themselves; they are proactive, and they have the capacity to persevere in the face of obstacles (Northouse, 2007). To successfully lead requires determination. Our goals are accomplished through constant determination. Leaders believe in their cause and are determined to make it happen. It requires enduring the journey in the face of enormous setbacks and obstacles. It takes commitment, patience, and persistence to achieve goals. This leadership journey is not a smooth road, but one filled with failure and disappointment. Abraham Lincoln, who is widely regarded as the greatest president in American history, was a pillar of determination. In spite of the enormous setbacks he faced, he kept focused on his goals. "With ordinary talent and extraordinary perseverance, all things are attainable," wrote Thomas Foxwell Buxton.

E for Emotional Intelligence (EI): *Leadership is about influencing human interactions* (Ignatius, 2013), which requires understanding and controlling of your emotions, as well as those of others. Decades of research now point to EI as the crucial factor that sets great leaders apart from the rest of the pack. It is a key component of effective leadership. It is learning to express yourself in a way that encourages good relationships through empathy and understanding.

Being emotionally intelligent includes the following skills, which are recognized as central to success in leadership and to your ability to manage change:

- ➲ **Self-Awareness**: The ability to understand your responses to situations and other people's feelings and emotions.

- ➲ **Self-Management**: The ability to harness emotions to facilitate cognitive activities as problem solving, and to motivate ourselves.

- ➲ **Social Awareness**: The ability to recognize and understand the feelings and emotions of others. This includes skills in empathy.

- ➲ **Relationship Management**: The ability to express your emotions and to communicate effectively.

EI plays a big part in effective communication. Leaders possessing high EI are able to communicate more effectively; therefore, influence and inspire others.

F for Flexibility. Flexibility promotes creativity and brings improvement. These leaders emphasize people above procedures. They are constantly surveying the environment; thus, recognizing the internal and external trends and adopting the necessary changes to remain current and effective while upholding their values. Organizations go through different cycles, and leaders that embrace flexibility are better able to transition their team through changes.

G for Gratitude: Leading with an attitude of gratitude allows one to appreciate the little contributions. Such leaders openly praise their team and publicly acknowledge their contributions. **Reward and Recognition** is important for building commitment and strengthening relationships. *"People work for money, but go the extra mile for recognition, praise, and rewards."* —Dale

Carnegie. Leaders must form relationships based on genuine respect, a sincere interest in seeing others succeed, and an appreciation for a variety of contributions to a goal (Axner, 1993).

H for Humility. Humility is a foundational leadership strength. True leaders always aim to serve rather than be served. Humble leaders use their power to empower others. They are able to genuinely relate to and empathize with their followers. They draw people by humility and honour, not by position and power. According to a study from the University of WashingtonFoster School of Business, *"humble people tend to make the most effective leaders."*

I for Inspiration: Inspirational Leadership is about energizing and creating a sense of direction and purpose for followers, and excitement and momentum to achieve goals. Inspirational leaders motivate their team to give of themselves and to strive to be their best. Such leaders create environments where people can do their best by instilling **Hope** and optimism. Inspirational leaders are capable of taking an organization and people to new heights. How you are able to inspire your team through your own actions and examples is an important component to achieving leadership success.

"The first task of a leader is to keep hope alive." —Joseph Batten

J for Jovial: A good attitude draws people to you. We want to be around such leaders having a great sense of **humour** because it is often an overlooked quality in leadership success. However, humour is a great way to win over and influence a team. It minimizes status distinctions between leaders and followers, and encourages interaction. Leaders who use humour allow people to feel comfortable around them. This acts as a catalyst to influence and inspire others.

K for Knowledge: Leaders are relied upon for their intelligence and skills, which determines the quality of the performance of the organization. They must show competence. To perform effectively, leaders need to be knowledgeable about their fields, in this regard in order to keep abreast of the ever changing environment, and to be able to make better informed decisions. Continuous learning is the most effective way for leaders to survive competition and manage change. When one stops learning, it is a sure sign of decline in one's leadership status.

L for Love: They have love for their fellowmen. **Mother Teresa** said it quite succinctly, *"It is not how much we do, but how much love we put in the doing. It is not how much we give, but how much love we put in the giving."* However, in today's self-seeking culture, love seems a taboo word in leadership. The Greek philosopher, Sophocles, said, "One word frees us of all the weight and pain of life. That word is love." Love is the fabric of life. Life without love is a subhuman kind of existence. There is a built-in need in us to receive love. But, just as much as we need to receive love, we also need to give love. We are not truly human if we cannot love. The tragic reality of this world is one of self-love, blind ambition, hatred, and corruption. As long as leaders allow themselves to be guided by the principles of selfishness, our world will degenerate. For a leader to maximize situations, this requires going beyond spreadsheets and routines. It's about taking a genuine interest in the team, which will include a common respect and appreciation for every individual. *"No one who is a lover of money, a lover of pleasure, or a lover of glory is a lover of man,"* wrote the Greek philosopher, Epictetus.

M for Management by Objectives: Setting strategic organizational objectives is the starting point. Management focuses on the set of processes that keep an organization functioning. Leadership on the other hand, requires the ability to influence a group toward the achievement of goals. Leadership relies on influence. There has never been a time in history when individuals who possess a blend of both leadership and management skills are more in demand. The great need for vision and inspirationis a must, but equally, systems must be monitored and controlled to ensure that tasks and road maps are created to operationalize the vision. Without efficient management skills, the direction set by a leader risks being unsustainable. Leadership is about change and achieving outcomes. If goals aren't attained, your leadership presence may be curtailed.

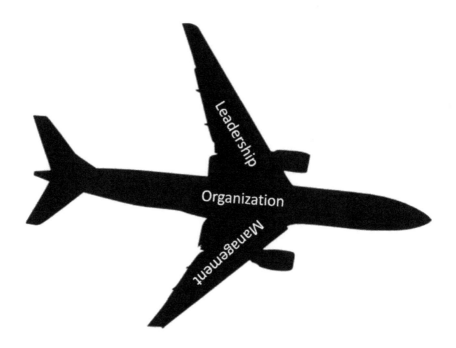

N for Noble: *The supreme quality for leadership is unquestionably* **Integrity**." —Dwight D. Eisenhower. Great leaders are known for the ethical principles they stand on, and their actions promote these values. They lead by example. They radiate moral authority, which is transferred down to the followers. Values are the beacons for finding the right direction and making ethical decisions. They are fair and promote justice. Leadership is not a right, but a privilege bestowed upon the leader by followers; of whom, much is given, much is required. Accountability is important for effective leadership. Leaders must make a conscious effort to take responsibility for their thoughts and actions. For them, having a high internal locus of control is superior to a high external locus of control (Nguyen, 2013).

Jose De La Vega was a successful merchant and philanthropist residing in 17th century Amsterdam. He became famous for his masterpiece Confusion of Confusions, the oldest book ever written on the stock exchange business. The book was written in Spanish; its original title is Confusión de Confusiones. Jose came up with four basic rules of the share market that are still of the greatest relevance today. The fourth rule was "He who wishes to become rich from this game must have both money and <u>patience</u>." Patience is the level of endurance one can take before negativity. It is also used to refer to the character trait of being steadfast. Sadly many leaders in today's world lack patience, and would rather trade in their integrity for short term gains.

O for Opportunity Seeking: Leaders focus on opportunities, not on problems. They don't sit and wait passively for something to happen or someone to act. They are proactive rather than reactive. They take action while others are waiting for a safer situation or assured results. Ordinary individuals see the glass as half empty while leaders view it as half full. They prepare and plan carefully. They believe once there is a will, there is a way, and they are determined to fashion it into being.

"Failure to recognize possibilities is the most dangerous and common mistake one can make." —Astronaut, Mae Jamison

P for Personal Development: Personal development (spiritual, emotional, mental, social, and physical) is crucial to leadership success. Leaders that embrace a growth mind-set know that leadership development is an ongoing process, so they are constantly looking for ways to improve themselves.

People give more importance to academic and professional achievement rather than to personal growth. This has caused a lot of emotional struggles. Brian Tracy stated, *"Personal development is a major time-saver. The better you become, the less time it takes you to achieve your goals."* Self-awareness is the platform for achieving higher levels of performance. You must be able to identify both your strengths and weaknesses. This is a vital part of a person's growth and maturity, and is much like how you nurture a plant.

"There is only one corner of the universe where you can be certain of improving, and that's your own self," —Aldous Huxley

Q for Quality: As Vince Lombardi stated, "The quality of a person's life is in direct proportion to their commitment to excellence regardless of their chosen field of endeavour." Leaders focus on creating excellence. A leader realizes that his finished product is a direct reflection of himself, so he always gives *100% to whatever he is trying to accomplish.* A dentist explained why his crowns are always flawless. Unlike some dentists, he said, I never have a problem with the crowns that come back from the lab. If I send them perfect work, they send me perfect crowns. This dentist doesn't worry about the end result. He focuses on his role in the initial stage of the process. Once the leader sets the example, everyone in the team will follow as well.

"Be a yardstick of quality. Some people aren't used to an environment where excellence is expected." —Steve Jobs

R for Risk Taking: Leadership is synonymous with change. Risk brings change and opportunity, but risk-taking comes at a cost and can take a long time to pay off. However, risk-taking is an indispensable part of leadership. When we look at leaders who are making a difference, we see that they have the courage to chart new paths. They take the necessary risks because they know that it is the only way forward. Creativity and Innovation are the lifeblood of any organization. The best leaders are calculated risk-takers. In recent years, more and more executives have embraced the point of view that failure is a prerequisite to invention. "The fastest way to succeed," IBM's Thomas Watson Sr. once said, "is to double your failure rate." The growing acceptance of failure is changing the way companies approach innovation.

S for Social Responsibility: Great leaders not only focus on the organization and their employees, but also, the society as a whole. They look at the overall big picture. Leadership is about making a meaningful contribution. They are concerned about the future and how their decisions will impact it. Leaders are responsible for fulfilling their civic duty; the actions of an individual must benefit the whole of society. This is why it important to give back to the society and our communities. Such leaders genuinely care about making a positive difference. They positively impact their organization, their communities, the overall society and that is how you leave a lasting legacy. Everybody wins.

John D. Rockefeller, (1839–1937), provided a prime example of how moving the focus from oneself to others can improve your life and that of others. In 1879, his company, Standard Oil, handled about 90 percent of the refining in the United States. By the age of 50, he was the richest man alive. But, in 1891, he had a nervous breakdown and was near death. However, he recovered from his illness in just a few months and spent the remaining 40 years of his life as a philanthropist. Early in the twentieth century, his personal fortune peaked at nearly $900 million. At the time of his death, his estate was valued at a little under $26 million. His donations did a lot of good in the world, and as for himself, he extended his life by nearly another fifty years, living to the age of 97.

T for Teach: Training and coaching—they are teachers. They train mentor and coach their team. They share their knowledge and wisdom. They help to develop and grow their team. As leaders, one of our primary roles is to support our people to realize their full potential. It's about understanding each of your team motivations and priorities, and enabling them to flourish and achieve their goals. Such leaders focus is on producing more leaders and not just more followers. They embrace succession planning.

U for Unite: Great leaders build great teams. They are able to rally people and gain support for their goals. They work by uniting and not by dividing. They need everyone on board and going in the same direction. Building bridges is their primary objective. They bring people together for the common good. They make an effort to understand others, their drivers, motivators, and value sets in order to truly give and get the best from them.

V for Visionary: The best leaders are able to create a vision that projects optimism and inspires others to work toward creating it. It's so clear and real that they infuse passion and energy into their work and those they lead. They paint a picture of the future that is captivating and compelling and, coupled with their talent and dedication, they convince and mobilize others to get on board. They see into the future and strive to take others there. "The very essence of leadership is that you have to have vision. *You can't blow an uncertain trumpet.*" —Theodore Hesburgh

W for Wisdom: *"Wisdom is the principal thing; therefore, get wisdom: and with all thy getting, get understanding"* —Proverbs 4:7. Wisdom is fundamental to leadership existence. Wisdom is the effective application of knowledge. It is discernment, discretion, understanding and foresight. Knowledge will only get you so far; it's wisdom that will give you the edge. Knowledge is knowing how to use a gun; wisdom is knowing when to use it and when to keep it holstered.

$$W = f(T + E)^y$$

Wisdom is a function of Time and Experience

Wisdom is a function of **Time** and **Experience** to the power of **You** (**Individual factors**). Individual factors comprise aptitude, motivation, attitude, personality, and cognitive style (the preferred way an individual processes information).

"It is better to lead from behind and to put others in front, especially when you celebrate victory when nice things occur. You take the front line when there is danger. Then, people will appreciate your leadership." —**Nelson Mandela**

X for X-Factor: Leadership requires being present in the right place and the right time. You may be a leader, but what also matters is whether you are in a position within which your talents can shine forth. Leadership is largely situational.

Leadership seems to emerge when a situation occurs that demands someone to take the helm. If Mahatma Ghandi had been born in a different era or country, would his skills have been effectively utilized?

Y for Youthful Balance and Wellbeing: Ultimately, your well-being is very important to your overall success as a leader. Unless you are healthy, you cannot lead your team with vitality and vigour. It's important to take care of your **Health**. Only when you take care of yourself, you can perform at your peak level and thus enjoy the fruits of your leadership.

Z for Zealous: "As Ralph Waldo Emerson said, "Enthusiasm is one of the most powerful engines of success....Nothing great was ever achieved without enthusiasm." It is enthusiasm that will energize you and propel your cause forward. The spirit of enthusiasm will lift you and those around you when the odds are stacked against you. Passion is indeed oxygen of the soul.

Alexander the Great, after conquering many kingdoms, was returning home. On the way, he fell ill and his generals took him to his death bed. With death staring him in his face, Alexander summoned his generals and told them his three ultimate wishes:

1.   The best doctors should carry his coffin.

2.   The wealth he has accumulated (money, gold, precious stones) should be scattered along the procession to the cemetery.

3.   His hands should be let loose, hanging outside the coffin for all to see.

One of his generals who was surprised by these unusual requests asked Alexander to explain.

Here is what Alexander the Great had to say:

I want the best doctors to carry my coffin to demonstrate that, in the face of death, even the best doctors in the world have no power to heal. I want the road to be covered with my treasure, so that everybody sees that material wealth acquired on earth stays on earth. I want my hands to swing in the wind, so that people understand that we come to this world empty handed and we leave this world empty handed after the most precious treasure of all is exhausted, and that is time.

The key to optimum living and leading is renewing yourself: physically, mentally, spiritually and emotionally. By embracing and applying these principles, you can effectively lead yourself and others. Remember, your Health is in your own hands; look after it. Wealth is only meaningful if you can share, and also, enjoy it while you are still alive and healthy. What you do for yourself dies with you, but what you do for others will live on. Strive to make a positive impact!

Conclusion

As a leader, situations are coming at you with full force for which you are totally unprepared; temptation is constantly knocking on your door and the critics are at your heels. **The Ultimate Leader: Learning, Leading and leaving a Legacy of Hope is a guidebook to performing at your optimum level**. It will Energize your Mind, Body & Soul and strengthen you for the journey ahead. The best leaders lead from the inside out. They practice holistic leadership. They lead with Authenticity, Humility, Integrity and Hope—The Pillars of Leadership. Leadership skills are perishable. How does one create a lasting legacy? It's through sowing seeds of hope. Hope is the lifeline that keeps people holding on. Long after these leaders have gone, they still continue to live on in the hearts and minds of followers. You too, can carve your footprints in stone by implementing the techniques and strategies outlined in this book. It is an impeccable roadmap to building and maintaining leadership effectiveness even in the midst of uncertainty.

References

Bums, J. M. (2003) Transforming leadership. NY: Atlantic Monthly Press.

Cerff, K. (2006). The role of hope, self-efficacy and motivation to lead in the development of leaders in theSouth African college student context. Doctoral Dissertation, Regent University, VA.

Forbes, S. (2011). Remembering 9/11: The Rudy Giuliani Interview. *Forbes Magazine*.

Goethals, G. R., Sorenson, G. J., & Burns, J. M. (Eds.), (2004). Hope. InEncyclopedia of leadership(Vol. 2, pp. 673-675). Thousand Oaks, CA: Sage Publications.

Hamel, G., & Prahalad, C. K. (2005). Strategic Intent. *Harvard Business Review*, 83 (7/8), 148-161.

Heber D. Vegetables, fruits and phytoestrogens in the prevention of diseases. J Postgrad Med. Apr-Jun 2004;50(2):145-9.

Ludema, J. D., Wilmot, T. B., & Srivastva, S (August, 1997). Organization hope: Reaffirming the constructive task of social and organizational inquiry. Human Relations, 50:8,1015-1053

Luthans, F., & Youssef, C. M. (2004). Investing in people for competitive advantage. Organizational Dynamics, 33:2, 143-160.15, 801-823

Mitchell H.H. (1945), "The Chemical Composition of the Adult and its bearing on the Biochemistry of Growth. Human Body," (Journal of Biological Chemistry 158

Snyder, C. R., Lopez, S. J., Shorey, H. S., Rand, K. L., & Feldman, D. B. (2003). Hope theory, measurements, and applications to school psychology. School Psychology Quarterly, 18(3), 122-139.

Epilogue

We have come to the end of this book. Thank you for staying with it. I hope you have known at all times that the author has your best interests in mind. **The Ultimate Leader: Learning, Leading, and Leaving a Legacy of Hope** gives strategies forbuilding and maintaining leadership effectiveness. It combines wisdom from the ages with the author's insights; thus, giving a winning formula for success.

May you apply these principles outlined in this book to perform at your optimum level. It has worked for many others and can do exactly the same for you.

I wish you the very best in life!

Sincerely,

Brigette